WILLIAM HUSKISSON AND LIBERAL REFORM

WILLIAM HUSKISSON AND LIBERAL REFORM

AN ESSAY ON THE CHANGES IN ECONOMIC POLICY IN THE TWENTIES OF THE NINETEENTH CENTURY

ALEXANDER BRADY

SECOND EDITION

Routledge
Taylor & Francis Group
LONDON AND NEW YORK

Published by
Routledge
by arrangement with Oxford University Press.
2 Park Square, Milton Park, Abingdon, Oxfordshire OX14 4RN
711 Third Avenue, New York, NY 10017

First issued in paperback 2014

Routledge is an imprint of the Taylor and Francis Group, an informa business

First Edition	**1928**
Second Edition	**1967**

ISBN 13: 978-0-714-61456-4 (hbk)
ISBN 13: 978-0-415-76044-7 (pbk)

Publisher's Note
The publisher has gone to great lengths to ensure the quality of this reprint but points out that some imperfections in the original may be apparent

INTRODUCTION TO THE SECOND EDITION

THE first edition of this monograph has been out of print for many years. There is still a demand for it. Copies seldom enter the market and are then highly priced. In view of these circumstances reprinting was thought desirable, even though revision and enlargement of the text was not practicable. It is, therefore, presented in its original form as an essay on the significant changes in commercial and imperial policy in the 1820's with which the name of Huskisson was associated.

Since the first edition of this book two volumes on Huskisson have appeared and are mentioned here as useful supplements: *The Huskisson Papers*, edited by Lewis Melville (London, 1931) and *Huskisson and His Age* by C. R. Fay (London, 1951). *The Huskisson Papers* is a selection of the statesman's correspondence, from his stay in Paris during the early period of the French Revolution to his death in 1830. In one respect the selection is disappointing: it contains few letters on the critical measures of policy with which he was concerned and which were debated intensely in the houses of parliament. It contains, however, some revealing letters on political practice in the pre-Reform era, the winning of elections, the formation of ministries, the distribution of patronage, and the constant intrigues and jealousies involved in the contests for place and power among members of the governing class. It also has letters showing Huskisson's wide and acute grasp of finance and commerce and the high opinion of his judgment on these matters entertained by colleagues. On Huskisson's political milieu and associates, however, more information is found in A. Aspinall's essay, "The Canningite Party", *Transactions of the Royal Historical Society*, Fourth Series, volume XVII (1934). Professor Aspinall traces in much detail the fortunes and misfortunes of the Canningite group within the Tory ranks. He illustrates convincingly a point cited in the introductory chapter of the present book that not until 1823 did Huskisson's intimate connection with Canning permit him to obtain a ministerial position which in the next four years enabled him to achieve distinguished reforms. It is fair to admit, however, that had Huskisson come to the Presidency of the Board of Trade much earlier it hardly follows that he could have carried the same measures. The temper and circumstances of the time now favoured the kind of enactments he sought. A period of reform succeeded a period of reaction; the social environment and currents of opinion in the 1820's were notably changing.

The late C. R. Fay, a memorable personality to academic friends in both England and Canada, acquired an impressive knowledge, perhaps unequalled in his day, of British commercial and imperial policy in the first half of the nineteenth century. His chief hero was Huskisson, whose life and times he undertook to write in two volumes. *Huskisson and His Age*, the only volume completed before his death, is at once fascinating and puzzling. It almost totally ignores the conventional rules of biography. No discernible logic but only a wayward fancy seems to dictate the order and arrangement of its contents. It opens with the dramatic death of Huskisson and only in the tenth chapter discusses his youth and education. The book illustrates again the comment of Fay's friend, Maynard Keynes, on an earlier volume that "in its immense disorder there are the qualities of a work of art". It is scarcely suitable for the undergraduate, at least until he has first acquired a knowledge of the period and perhaps read an earlier book by Fay, *The Corn Laws and Social England*. But with this reservation it is to be strongly recommended as a rewarding study. Most of its chapters are separate and enlightening tours in the social, political, and economic byways of Huskisson's age. Fay did not neglect the permanent officials who contributed to the story of reform. He paid special tribute to the formidable figure of James Deacon Hume, Huskisson's trusted ally and admirer at the Custom House, whose codification of the custom laws facilitated their reform.

Fay's gleanings in manuscripts turn up interesting items. He finds, for example, a discerning contemporary assessment of Huskisson's major reforms by Kirkman Finlay in a letter of 1826 to John Gladstone, William Ewart Gladstone's father: "It is very cruel in Baring and some other persons who ought to know better to press the Government and mainly Mr. Huskisson with the attacks they do . . . that the present ministers have done more good to trade and manufactures by the new principles they have introduced and acted on than any Ministry which has preceded them, no rational man can deny. But the rational men are quiet and say little, while the noise and nonsense get possession of the fools, who will in all kingdoms form an immense majority".

It is hardly necessary to re-emphasize that Huskisson's reforms when President of the Board of Trade were directly related to deep changes in British commercial and industrial life, the progress of inventions, the growing political power of the middle class, and a fresh outlook on the assets and liabilities of colonies which was influenced not merely by the mounting pressures within Britain's Second Empire, but indirectly by the disruption of the Spanish and Portuguese empires in South America and the opportunities thus afforded for British trade. These and allied factors continued to exert an influence in the twenty odd years after Huskisson left Wellington's ministry.

The chief governing idea in Huskisson's statecraft was that of an imperial economy, sustained not as in the past by monopoly but by preferential tariffs, and bolstered by regulations that would permit both colonies and metropolis to augment their wealth through trade with other nations on a basis of reciprocity. The idea had critics among those who wanted no interference with long-established regulations and those who wanted different devices more favourable to their own vested interests. But the British and colonial commercial classes generally welcomed the reforms. A Halifax newspaper saw the new colonial freedom introduced by Huskisson as creating "a generous flame of enthusiastic and patriotic joy". Yet the important fiscal preferences, such as those on timber, corn, and sugar, primarily benefited the products of the British North American and West Indian colonies. They were not extended to the then small and remote settlements in Australia and South Africa, although in 1825 Mauritius was granted the same preference for its sugar as the West Indies. Some preferences were more prized in the colonies than others. The timber preference was not merely highly controversial in Britain but evidently for Canada a mixed blessing. There its critics asserted that it led to ill-planned and wasteful exploitation of the forest and discouraged the best forms of settlement.[1]

In the quarter century after Huskisson's major measures British and colonial opinion on policy was in a state of flux. The dynamism of economic growth and change was creating a variety of new pressures and new views. In the advanced colonies the growing impulse for self-government produced an insistent demand for regulation of their tariffs and trade, not by the imperial parliament, but by the colonial legislatures. The colonists generally had no quarrel with the Huskisson idea of an imperial economy, but with the manner whereby it was run. They protested that their interests were impaired by the fiscal and other restraints imposed by the authorities in London. In response to these requests, Lord Stanley, then Secretary

[1] See Adam Shortt, *Imperial Preferential Trade* (Toronto, 1904), 25-6; also Klaus E. Knorr *British Colonial Theories 1570-1850* (Toronto, 1944), 325-9.

of State for the Colonies in Peel's ministry, in a despatch to the West Indian colonies of July 30, 1842, declared that since the Government was satisfied with the results of Huskisson's legislation it intended to give fuller effect to the spirit in which it was conceived. This it did, not by conceding control to the colonies, but by removing certain restrictions on colonial industry, reducing duties on colonial imports, and thus helping to fortify the commercial bonds between colonies and metropolis. In the same spirit it revised in the Canada Grain Act of 1843 the old sliding scale of duties so as to admit Canadian wheat and flour at nominal rates. Flour derived from American wheat imported to and ground in Canada was admitted at the same rate, a concession that quickly helped to double the milling capacity of the Canadas and increased traffic on the St. Lawrence waterway.

In the early 1840's, therefore, the Huskisson system was still substantially intact. Its few modifications might be considered as extensions in harmony with its ethos. Yet by 1850 its basic features were being swept away by the rapid march of free trade. For the North American colonies and especially for the particular interests that benefited from the preferences, the abolition of the Corn Laws in 1846 was a decisive shock that made them realise a new era in empire economics had begun. The chapter opened by Huskisson and his associates was now being closed, and a different type of imperial economy was to develop. The colonists perhaps should not have been so surprised and staggered by what had happened. The progress of preferences in recent years was but the logical forerunner of a fuller free trade. Significantly on the heels of the abolition of the Corn Laws, Lord John Russell's Government in 1846 permitted the colonies to repeal the restrictions on their commerce under the Possessions Act and three years later itself repealed the Navigation Act. The colonists could henceforth trade where they liked, with whom they liked, and in whatever ships they liked. These new freedoms were some compensation for the preferences they lost.

It is scarcely relevant here to probe the influences underlying this profound change in imperial policy or to speculate on whether some elements of the Huskisson system might advantageously have been retained. We may simply add that in Britain the fervent advocacy of free trade tended to reduce interest in the empire. In so far as such an interest survived among fiscal reformers it was expressed in the opinion that the material welfare of the colonies could best be achieved through the removal of protection. What was beneficial for Britain was beneficial for them. The advocates of this view looked to the day when members of the empire would all be amicably bound together, not by imperial preferences, but by imperial free trade. Their vision was never, of course, to be realised, for the larger colonies soon discovered that they needed protective tariffs to nourish their own industries even at the expense of Britain. The maintenance of a satisfactory preferential system would doubtless have encountered more and more difficulty in reconciling the diverse interests of colonies and metropolis. There the matter must be left. This book concerns only the initial steps to freer trade and the imperial preferences and other devices whereby it might become a reality. It is the story of a transition.

A.B.

University of Toronto
July 13, 1966.

PREFACE TO THE FIRST EDITION

THIS book does not profess to be a biography of William Huskisson. It is an 'essay'—an attempt to survey the changes in economic policy with which Huskisson, more than any other public man, was intimately connected. I am concerned with showing their character and the influences which brought them about. The importance of these changes lies in the fact that they formed an integral part in the fall of British mercantilism.

I should like to acknowledge the help which I have received from many friends. Among these I would specially mention Professor W. P. M. Kennedy, University of Toronto, who first suggested the subject and has helped me throughout; Professor R. M. MacIver, Professor C. R. Fay, and my other colleagues in the University of Toronto; Mr. Kenneth Bell, Balliol College, Oxford; the librarians and archivists of various libraries where I have worked, especially those of the Dominion Archives, Ottawa. I need scarcely say that for the conclusions and defects I take full responsibility.

A. B.

UNIVERSITY OF TORONTO.

January 1928.

CONTENTS

I

POLITICAL CAREER AND PARTY ALINEMENTS

THE career of William Huskisson contained no strands of drama. Few incidents of his life touch the imagination. His character in action had nothing of Canning's glittering éclat. Nor had his career the interest that may be found in that of Peel, who from the outset seemed to move along a road of brilliant accomplishments. The biographical sketch of Huskisson in this chapter is valuable, not for dramatic incidents, but in illustrating how events influenced the development of his ideas, and how party alinements shaped his accomplishments.

Son of a country gentleman, not above the middle class, Huskisson was born in 1770 near Wolverhampton. It is of slight interest that as a boy he attended the schools of Brewood in Staffordshire, Albrighton in the same county, and Appleby in Leicestershire. More interesting is it that he early gave evidence of excellent mathematical ability, later to mature into an enviable capacity for the handling of financial questions. His departure to Paris in 1783 was the one event of prime importance in his boyhood. In the French capital his education was directed by a celebrated and somewhat odd uncle, Dr. Gem, who had wide intellectual pursuits and a keen interest in political and social movements. Among his many acquaintances in France were the distinguished Americans, Franklin and Jefferson. It was in many respects fortunate that Huskisson should come under the tutorship of the versatile Gem in the electric atmosphere of pre-revolutionary France. In Gem's home he came into contact with men of ideas, and in the French capital he found a veritable furnace of political discussion. From 1783–89 the tottering French monarchy was adopting every available expedient to stall off bankruptcy. Such an event provided Parisians with the occasion for political thinking, and the exchange of ideas could not but influence young Huskisson's mind. In the opening stages of the Revolution he was not merely an interested spectator, but in a very slight degree an actor. He was elected a member of an association of moderates, the 'Club of 1789'. No evidence exists to prove that he took an absorbing part in the club's discussions, but he at least read before it a paper which has the interest of being the first statement of his ideas on public finance, a field later to become peculiarly his own.[1] The argument was not elaborately developed. Its general conclusion was the inexpediency of establishing a paper currency, a position from which Huskisson never retreated in his later career. The famous Report of the Bullion Committee in 1810, in part the work of Huskisson, was an expanded treatment of the theme of his juvenile paper. As a youth in revolutionary France he had thus grappled with an important question later to engage his energies as a prominent English parliamentarian, and his view then was quite as emphatic as that later adopted in the House of Commons. So strongly was he opposed to a paper currency that on the issue of the assignats he withdrew from the 'Club of 1789'. His interest in the Revolution ceased on his conviction of the fallacy in its political economy. Soon after this, in 1791, he became secretary to Lord Gower, British ambassador to France, and thereby laid the basis of a friendship that proved helpful in his future political career. On Gower's recall to England in August 1792 Huskisson accompanied him, and his nine years sojourn in France closed.

The precise influence of France upon Huskisson is difficult to determine. But it is not a little significant that one of the men destined to assist in guiding Great Britain into a new future should have been the spectator in France of events which aided in making the new future imperative. His residence in a country suffering, among other ills, from financial disorders, drove him to think upon currency and kindred problems, later to absorb much of

[1] Huskisson, *Speeches*, iii, pp. 641 ff. (3 vols. London, 1831).

his attention in British public life. His brochure read before the 'Club of 1789' is evidence of the fact. In addition, the hectic atmosphere of pre-revolutionary and revolutionary Paris could not but provide a political tutorship of supreme value. Huskisson witnessed a state passing rapidly through the shocks of revolutionary change. He saw elaborate experiments in legislation built on revolutionary logic. He was the spectator of efforts to attain definite social and political adjustments along lines of prescribed principles. He had the opportunity of seeing the latent weakness in the devastating method of revolution. Upon an impressionable mind such experience would inevitably leave its impress. It taught him the value of constructive reform and contributed greatly to the development of his reforming mind. It gave him a direction and a method. Too mentally balanced, perhaps too Anglo-Saxon, to be unduly swayed by the idealism of the Revolution, he yet learned from the drama of those intense years the meaning and need of a sober statesmanship. Later in his career he declared that, 'it is the business of a statesman to move onwards with the new combinations which have grown around him'. He must be prepared 'to make himself acquainted with facts—to watch events—to understand the actual situation of affairs, and the course of time and circumstances, as bearing upon the present state of his own country and the world'.[1] He must satisfy political needs as they arise, and not shrink from reform merely because it was innovation. Neither must he build upon abstract ideas, with no consideration of pre-existing interests or settled sentiments. The French Revolution had taught Huskisson that real statesmanship consisted in preserving and destroying; pruning away all that was decayed and invigorating what remained.

Soon after his return from France Huskisson began an apprenticeship in British politics. For a time he remained in the household of Lord Gower, where he made the acquaintance of Pitt which opened his political future. Through Pitt's influence he obtained a new office created

[1] *Speeches*, iii. 437.

under the Alien Act for making arrangements with French *émigrés*. About the same time he met the brilliant man with whose name and party he was later associated, George Canning. Canning with his tinselled and sterling talents —he possessed an abundance of both—had in 1793 made his début in the Commons and was already giving promise of political success. In winning Canning's friendship Huskisson fixed his future party connexions. Under the great name of Pitt he made his entrance to politics and underwent training in the political questions of the time. With Pitt's lineal successor, Canning, he was even more closely associated, and with him he was destined to carry on those traditions of reform which Pitt left as an inheritance to his successors. In 1795 Pitt moved him into the Under Secretaryship at War, vacated by Sir Evan Nepean. The office was not a sinecure. Dundas was the nominal secretary, but Dundas's energies were absorbed in the work for which he had singular capacity—the control of the Commons and the disposal of patronage. The most noteworthy of Huskisson's labours was the direction of arrangements for Sir Charles Grey's unfortunate expedition to the West Indies. The efficiency with which he accomplished his task won him the praise of his colleagues.

In 1796 Lord Carlisle procured him the representation of Morpeth, and his parliamentary career began. At first he failed to make any noticeable display in Parliament. Indeed, it appears that he did not deliver his maiden speech until February 1798. The fact is that he had few of the oratorical talents requisite at the time for parliamentary success and was content to make no attempts to acquire them. He pursued with diligence his secretarial duties until in 1800 on Pitt's resignation over the Catholic question, he retired from office, and the first period of his administrative career closed. Up to this date the one political fact of importance was his association with Pitt and his friendship with Canning. In 1802 he unsuccessfully contested Dover, and as a consequence remained out of Parliament until 1804. In this year Pitt drew him into his second ministry as Secretary to the Treasury, where under the Prime Minister he obtained a careful training in public finance. Pitt's second ministry, although strong on the Treasury bench, had little consistency and crumbled when Pitt died. During the brief and bizarre career of the Ministry of all the Talents Huskisson and his associate, Canning, moved aimlessly in opposition, but on the formation of the Portland Government in 1807 he was again in office as Secretary to the Treasury, with Canning as Minister for Foreign Affairs. All readers of English history know the vexatious events culminating in the dissolution of the Portland Cabinet: the differences between Castlereagh and Canning over the Convention of Cintra, the attack on the Duke of York, the expedition of Sir John Moore, and the future of Portugal. The climax was reached with the historic, if unedifying, duel between Canning and Castlereagh. Huskisson, although not directly implicated in the quarrel, followed his colleague from office, a demonstration of his close political association with Canning. We may indeed consider the two men as already leaders of the Liberal wing of the Tory party.

The division of the Tories into two bodies of opinion was one of the most important facts respecting party organization between 1810–30. Within parties, cleavage on policy is an inevitable and ordinary phenomenon. Frequent readjustment of principles to changing needs is necessary if a party is to exercise a vital influence on the life of a state. But there are always those ready to prevent an alteration in principles, as there are those desirous of accelerating change. The one group, clinging to those things which formerly won triumphs for the party, maintains obsolete watchwords and threadbare shibboleths. The other section, weary of worshipping old gods, is eager to shed much of its past and to enter the wilderness to win for the party a rebaptism, a new name and a new creed. The followers of Canning were such a group. During the war the differences between them and the larger wing of Tory opinion were not pronounced. Issues then were war issues. The triumph of British arms was the objective sought by all elements. Yet even before the close of the war it was evident that those who followed Canning were assuming an attitude different from that of other Tories. A perusal of the parliamentary debates of the period is convincing proof that the division existed.

The Canningites—Canning, Huskisson, Sturgis Brown—were in fact becoming what their later name so adequately describes, Liberal Tories. Liberal Toryism drew its chief inspiration from the younger Pitt of the period 1783–92: the Pitt who lived on visions of reform and who had hopefully looked forward to innumerable ameliorations in existing conditions, believing that there was 'a continued course of successive improvement in the general order of the world'.[1] Canning never ceased to confess that his most reliable guide in political affairs was Pitt. In his famous Liverpool speech of 1812 he declared that: 'to one man I was devoted with all my soul. Since the death of Mr. Pitt I acknowledge no leader; my political allegiance lies buried in his grave'.[2] The Canningites drew inspiration from Pitt for the carrying of financial and fiscal reform. Like Pitt in 1800, they championed the claims of the Catholics, although the larger body of Tories were uncompromisingly opposed to any concessions. Above all they adopted Pitt's flexible attitude towards political change in general, an attitude best described in Burke's lucid words as 'the disposition to preserve and the ability to improve taken together'. They believed that a position of immobility exposed the state to as much danger as did a policy of frequent change. Constructive statecraft consisted in a discriminating view of existing conditions, and a willingness to concede reform under the pressure of real need and strong opinion. Brougham had in mind this attitude when he remarked that 'Canning's principles were above the prejudices of the bigots who have rendered Toryism ridiculous'. The Canningites depended largely for their support upon the middle classes of which most of them were members. The so-called 'bigots', or High Tories, drew their strength from the Church and the land;

[1] Speech, 17 Feb. 1792.

[2] Phillips, W. A., *George Canning*, p. 60 (London, 1905).

their Toryism consisted in maintaining the privileges of the one and in advancing the interests of the other.

The High Tories had a simple and consistent creed. Eldon, who moved in the highest altitudes of Tory opinion, deprecated concessions to the demands of reform on the ground that such concessions, instead of satisfying existing needs, created further demands. So-called reform was followed by further change, and such a process would eventually dissolve the existing society. Political health could only be found in the preservation of the *status quo*. Such was the tone that Eldon gave to Toryism in the first quarter of the nineteenth century. His attitude towards change was remarkable for its consistency. He would obstruct the building of a railway for much the same reason as he opposed Catholic emancipation: it destroyed existing conditions and endangered the organic nature of society. If we grant the Whig bias of Brougham's judgement, there is truth in his observation that such as Eldon was 'when he left Oxford, such he continued above sixty years later, to the close of his long and prosperous life—the enemy of all reform, the champion of the throne and the altar, and confounding every abuse that surrounded the one or grew within the precincts of the other with the institutions themselves'.[1] Toryism, because of its fixed opposition to change, failed to make the proper distinction between the abuses of an institution and the institution itself. It stood unequivocably for political immobility.

The departure of Canning and Huskisson from the Portland ministry was an event of considerable moment. In the succeeding period the field of action was open for the uncompromising Tories of the Eldonian type. Thirteen years elapsed before the Canningites again had a ponderable influence in Tory councils. In 1814 Huskisson received the Commissionership of Woods and Forests, but it was an office very much below his capacity and brought little political influence. Canning, although maintaining a benevolent attitude towards the Perceval

[1] Brougham, *Historical Sketches of Statesmen who flourished in the time of George III*, p. 61, 2nd series, (London, 1839).

and Liverpool ministries, refused office until 1816, when he accepted the presidency of the Board of Control. The Tories of privilege were triumphant, and the composition of the Liverpool ministry in 1812 bore witness to their triumph. Its character and history between 1812–22 were those of a reactionary government. It was formed primarily as a war administration, and Canning might have been its Secretary for Foreign Affairs but for his disdainful opposition to Castlereagh's leadership in the House of Commons. His haughty refusal to bow before anything like party organization under men whose personalities and policies he disliked had the result of excluding from office his immediate followers, most prominent among whom was Huskisson. Had Canning accepted, Huskisson, it was rumoured, would have become Chancellor of the Exchequer. But these plans came to nought, and the Government contained no men of Liberal leanings.

The year 1822 is a turning-point. A number of political coincidences opened the way to reform. The session of 1821 had provided abundant evidence of the ministry's weakness in Parliament and in the country. Liverpool was, therefore, concerned with patching up his shaky structure. An opportunity was given him when Sidmouth, realizing that there were no longer seditions to be discovered, retired from the Home Office. 'The truth is', he declared 'that it was because my official bed was become comparatively a bed of roses that I determined to withdraw from it. When strewn with thorns, I would not have left it.'[1] His confession was evidence that the need for High Toryism had passed, and that something more than sedition-hunting was requisite. Liverpool moved the young Peel, whose tireless energy had already made an impression on his contemporaries, into the vacancy. His accession brought debating weight to the Government and a reforming mind to the Home Office. Other allies were found in the Whig group of the Grenvilles. They were wooed and won in the conventional way, by the distribution of appointments.

[1] Sidmouth, quoted in Martineau, Harriet, *History of England During the Thirty Years Peace*, i. 279 (London, 1849).

Wits in the period stated that everything had fallen in price except the Grenvilles. Whatever their price, Liverpool believed that he must have their attachment, since it would weaken the Whigs and at the same time strengthen his own party.

But the most influential change in the ministry came in the autumn of 1822. On 12 August Castlereagh com mitted suicide—a political event of the first magnitude. Spencer Walpole goes so far as to describe it as one of the most important incidents in the history of the century. 'Londonderry is a great loss to his party,' wrote Grenville, 'he was considered one of the best managers of the House of Commons who ever sat in it.' [1] There lay his power and the Tory loss. High Toryism had lost its most dexterous and conciliatory parliamentary manager. The choice of a successor was momentous, for on it would depend very largely whether the policy of reaction would give way to reform. When George IV's deep-rooted dislike was at length overcome, Canning was moved into Castlereagh's place, and Brougham was afforded the opportunity to remark that 'Canning succeeds to Foreign Office, lead of the House, &c.—in short, all of Castlereagh except his good judgement, good manners and bad English.' [2]

With Canning in office Huskisson soon obtained a post of importance. A Tory later wrote that Canning 'embraced nearly all the principles of the Whigs and Radicals. He was prevented from agreeing with the latter on parliamentary reform by his previous speeches, but on almost every other point he went with them, so far as regarded general principle. On being entrusted with the command, he carried over the army to the enemy.' [3] Vansittart, Chancellor of the Exchequer since 1812, considered by some Tories as a millstone about the ministry's neck, retired and was succeeded by Robinson, who had been President of the Board of Trade. Huskisson, drawn from the obscurity of his Commissionership of Woods and Forests,

1 *Memoirs*, 44–5 (New York, 1875).
2 Maxwell, H., *The Creevey Papers*, ii. 49 (2 vols. London, 1904).
3 *Blackwood's*, June, 1827.

held since 1814, became in April 1823 President of the Board of Trade with a promise of ultimately entering the Cabinet. The great period of his career now began.

From 1809 when with Canning he had left Portland's ministry, he had steadily risen to prominence as an authority on financial questions, to which his position on the Bullion Committee of 1810, his part in the bullion debates of 1811, and again in those of 1819 bear witness. In 1816 he had been described by a keen observer as the ablest of the Canningites.[1] In the years previous to 1819 his dexterous marshalling of financial arguments frequently preserved the Liverpool ministry from defeat. The agriculturists and the Whigs found in him the most redoubtable debater on economic matters. But his entrance to the Board of Trade was to mark the real beginnings of his constructive work. He was destined in the succeeding years 'to raise his department to a consequence before unknown', and to initiate those reforms which give him a place amongst the leading British statesmen of the century. In February 1823 he was elected member for Liverpool. In the succeeding years the mercantile interests of his constituency greatly influenced his policy, and in his measures for the promoting of British trade they gave him special support and strong encouragement.

The infusion of such new blood strengthened and liberalized Liverpool's ministry. It is noteworthy that nearly half of the Cabinet members now sat in the House of Commons, while in 1815 more than three-fourths had been peers. The Government had become more representative of the middle and mercantile classes, and from them came the impulse for reform. The reaction against reform which characterized Eldonian Conservatism began to break, and although the Chancellor remained on the Woolsack until 1827, he was unable to maintain his hitherto dominant influence. With the entrance of the Canningites to the Liverpool ministry the first real chapter of English reform in the nineteenth century opened. Peel in the

[1] Bagot, Josceline, *George Canning and His Friends*, ii. 27 (2 vols. London, 1909).

Home Office, Huskisson in the Board of Trade, Robinson under Huskisson's guidance at the Exchequer, struck out boldly on new paths and carried measures that entitle the ministry to rank amongst the great reforming administrations of the century.

The period of reform following the reconstruction of the Cabinet illustrates the truism that party policy and philosophy are generally determined by the manner in which the constituent elements of a party combine. The Liberal element among the Tories had succeeded in obtaining the upper hand. Yet the Government rested on a very unstable base. The elements within it were so diverse in their general views that the ministry proved little more than a coalition. From the outset the question of Catholic emancipation was a rock of difficulty. The Canningites, in accordance with the tradition inherited from Pitt, favoured emancipation. Eldon and the ultra-Tories were adamant in their opposition. A compromise was reached to the effect that in the ministry the Catholic question should remain, as it had since 1812, an open one. Notwithstanding this arrangement it continued to be the touchstone of differences between the party elements. Other subjects arose to threaten ministerial disintegration. A writer in *Blackwood's* stated that if properly united in principle and personal feeling the ministry would 'be powerful beyond all precedent', but due to its lack of union it acted as though it did not know how to maintain itself in office.[1]

The perilously strange nature of the incompatible blendings within the party is forcibly illustrated by the election of 1826. Palmerston, Secretary at War, whose sympathies were with the Canningites and emancipation, ran at Cambridge against Goulburn, Chief Secretary for Ireland, and Copley Attorney-General. All the ultra-Tory forces were exerted for the defeat of Palmerston and his removal from the ministry on the ground of his Liberal and Catholic leanings. Huskisson's commercial policy also tended to alienate the more advanced upholders of the *status quo*

[1] *Blackwood's*, August, 1825.

and to widen the breach with the Canningites. Only the consummate tact of Liverpool kept the ministry together, and even he in December 1826 doubted whether it would meet Parliament in the succeeding February. His illness in the spring of 1827 sounded the death-knell of the Coalition Government that he had so long preserved. Inevitable distintegration took place. Canning in the noon-day brightness of his genius was unable to hold together for a month the Government that the so-called 'arch-mediocrity' had maintained for years. Wellington once remarked that Canning's temper was enough to blow him up. Dislike of his temper, dislike of his brilliant talents, and dislike of the principles for which his group stood led to a large secession of Tories: Bathurst, Melville, Westmorland, Bexley, Wellington, and Peel.

The accession of Canning to a ministry purged of advanced Tories was a Liberal triumph. It seemed that the reforms begun by Huskisson and Canning would now be carried to completion. The ultra-Tory *Blackwood's* viewed events with undisguised dread and found a suitable parallel for them in past history:

'If the question were put to us, we could not confidently say that the English revolution has not commenced—that we are not in its first stages—that the same characteristics cannot be found in this country which distinguished the beginning of the French revolution. We have reached the point when the government has embraced the destructive doctrines of the economists and philosophers—and has thrown itself for support upon the Democrats and Infidels.' [1]

Yet, as Greville observed, no man took office under more embarrassing circumstances than Canning. The ministry was unable to stand upon its own feet without the support of the Whigs, and their entrance brought all the weaknesses of a fusionist government. The Whig, Lansdowne entered the Cabinet without office. Tierney accepted the Mint. Brougham refused office, but his formidable, if erratic, debating power was on Canning's side. A Canningite government was not his ideal of perfection, but he pre-

[1] *Blackwood's*, June, 1827.

ferred it to one of an Eldonian complexion. To Creevey he wrote: ' "Lock the door on Eldon and Co." and this can only be done by joining Canning.' One is reminded of O'Connell's felicitous explanation for joining the Whigs: 'A Whig government is like Paddy's old hat stuck in a broken pane; it is true that it does not let in much light, but it at least keeps out the cold.' But the Whig party as a body did not swing to the support of Canning. Grey in the Lords remained coldly in opposition. He had long opposed Canning on personal as well as on political grounds. He was not prepared to change the attitude which he had assumed in 1809 when he had remarked that 'he was against proscription in forming an administration, yet Canning was the last man that he would unite with'. In 1827 his voice of criticism joined the chorus of the disaffected Tories.

Whatever might be its parliamentary strength, Canning's ministry had abundance of talent. Among its members were Lyndhurst as Lord Chancellor, Huskisson as Treasurer of the Navy and President of the Board of Trade, Palmerston as Secretary at War, and William Lamb as Irish Secretary. Had its career not been untimely cut short, it might have marked a real turning-point in the history of British politics. Canning might have anticipated Disraeli in constituting a party on Conservative instead of Tory principles, and Huskisson as President of the Board of Trade might have anticipated the great financial reforms of Peel. But after reaching the zenith of his ambition, Canning held office for merely three months. His death dissolved his already weak Government and destroyed the hopes of a reconstituted Toryism.

It is worth drawing special attention to the fact that Huskisson held in Canning's brief ministry the same office, President of the Board of Trade, as he had held in the previous administration. He made clear his reason for doing so in a letter to John Hope: 'the measures which I have brought forward on the part of Government, as President of the Board of Trade, have been much attacked; fresh attacks are announced, and I am unwilling to quit a threatened post, if for no other reason, for this, that it is so threatened.'[1]

The chief events following Canning's death were connected with the ill-starred Goderich ministry, in which an attempt was made to establish an administration of the Liberal-Tory character. The preferences and interferences of the King considerably injured its prospects at the outset, and the weakness of Goderich brought its dissolution. 'Never surely', wrote Huskisson, 'was there a man at the head of affairs so weak, undecided and utterly helpless.'[2] The fall of Goderich signalized the failure of attempting to constitute a fusionist cabinet of Canningites and Whigs. The Duke of Wellington, repudiator of Canningitism, undertook to form an administration.

Wellington was quick in visualizing the situation. He concluded that it would be difficult to constitute a government wholly of ultra-Tories. Hence, to give debating and administrative strength to his ministry, he made proffers to Huskisson and his followers, and once more a fusionist government of the Liverpool character was formed. Huskisson obtained the office which he had chosen in the Goderich ministry in preference to the Exchequer, the Colonial Secretaryship, described by Ellenborough as an office of 'great labour and importance'. He chose this post because of his growing interest in the Empire. The other Canningites were variously distributed: Dudley became Minister for Foreign Affairs, Palmerston Secretary at War, Charles Grant President of the Board of Trade, and William Lamb, 'a Whig in name . . . but a Canningite in deed', Secretary for Ireland.

The manifold difficulties in a fusion of ultra-Tories and Liberal Tories were soon evident. The new ministry had scarcely been organized before it was rent by internal discords over foreign policy, the corn laws, and parliamentary reform. Ellenborough remarked of the first Cabinet meeting that 'the courtesy was that of men who have just fought

[1] Huskisson to John Hope, 20 Apr. 1827. Additional MS. 38749, f.205 b (British Museum).

[2] Huskisson to Lord Granville, 8 Jan. 1828. Add. MS. 38754, f.50 b.

a duel'.[1] Huskisson in combining with Wellington presumed that since the duke had accepted him and the other Canningites, he and his colleagues would not be required to surrender their policies. Soon after the formation of the Wellington ministry he wrote to Lord Granville:

'I trust that in looking over the enclosed list, in which Dudley remains where he is, a pledge of Canning's foreign policy—Grant where he is, a pledge to the policy with which, when I was at the Board of Trade, I was more particularly connected—Palmerston, the catholic representative of Cambridge—and myself in our respective situations, that I shall not be accused of deserting Mr. Canning's principles.'[2]

But a conflict with Wellington over the policy of the Government quickly developed. Within a few weeks Huskisson offered to resign because of an irritating difference over a corn law. He wished no departure from the principles enunciated in the Corn Bill of the previous year. Wellington on the other hand, with many of his followers, was partial to a measure more favourable to the agriculturists upon whom the High Tories relied for support. Thus the division within the Tory party was really between those who represented the industrial interests of the middle-class and those who stood for the agrarian interests of the landed aristocracy.

The question of parliamentary representation also ruffled the peace of Cabinet deliberations. The shameless corruption in the boroughs of Penryn and East Retford convinced the Government that their representatives should be transferred either to the neighbouring Hundreds or to unrepresented towns. The ultra-Tories favoured the transference of the seats to the neighbouring Hundreds where the landed classes still exercised control. Huskisson and his followers, convinced that more adequate representation was due to the industrial, commercial, and middle classes, favoured the transference of the seats to large towns, although they were willing to compromise by yielding the seats of one borough to the Hundreds. In a division on the

[1] Ellenborough's *Diary* i. 3 (London, 1881).
[2] Huskisson to Lord Granville, 18 Jan. 1828. Add. MS. 38754, f. 162 b.

issue Huskisson and Palmerston voted against the Government. The former with unwarrantable hastiness, wrote an ill-worded letter to Wellington offering his resignation 'if the Duke thought that his continuance in office would be inconvenient to the public service'. Wellington, probably glad of an occasion for getting rid of a troublesome colleague, accepted the letter as a resignation, and Huskisson, followed by other leading Canningites—Palmerston, Dudley, and Lamb—left the ministry. 'We have now', wrote Greville, 'a Tory Government, and all that remained of Canning's party are gone.'[1] The ultras in the Tory Cabinet had dropped the Liberals. *Blackwood's* in a leading article expressed the exulting joy of ultra-Toryism:

'We have at last, thank God, got rid of the Liberals, and once more have the happiness to live under a pure Tory Government. Not a remnant, we rejoice to say of that bastard political sect, that Canning, cowardly, compromising, conciliatory school has been left to divide and weaken the measures of the Cabinet.'[1]

Huskisson's breach with Wellington meant the virtual end of his political career. During the two remaining years of his life he maintained on most questions an attitude of benevolence towards the administration. But it was evident that the Tory party had ceased to hold his allegiance. Had he lived through the party turmoil of the thirties it is probable that he would have accompanied Palmerston and Lamb in manœuvring into the ranks of the newer Whigs. According to Greville, Brougham, at the time of Huskisson's fatal accident in 1830, was on his way to Liverpool and hoped there to sign a treaty bringing Huskisson into a new combination made up of moderate Whigs and enlightened Tories. It is likely, had he failed to join Brougham's wing of the Whigs, that he would have assisted in the construction of a strong rival party outside the Tory ranks. He might thus have possibly anticipated in some degree the work of Gladstone in the creation of a Liberal party. Indeed he and his followers already wore

[1] *Journal*, 110.
[2] *Blackwood's*, July, 1828.

the tag of 'Liberal'. In August 1830 he wrote to Sir James Graham, then a Whig with a political future:

'The present ministry ought not to stand the shock of the next session, and it is the interest of all public men—I might say the interest of the public as well as of the party—that they should come to an understanding not to listen to any separate overture for reinforcing it, unless upon the preliminary admission of an entire reconstruction.'[1]

Huskisson would gladly have placed a new party on the political anvil.

Upon the absorbing issue of the time, parliamentary reform, he drifted from the former Canningite position. Canning always had remained frigidly hostile to any real measure of parliamentary reform. As on all occasions, he had polished phrases in explanation, 'the balance is now perhaps as nearly poised as human wisdom can adjust it. I fear to touch that balance, the disturbance of which must bring confusion on the nation.'[2] On this subject Canning was as rigid as Eldon, and Huskisson's views previous to 1828 were similar. But in the two years preceding his death he was shedding the fixity of the Canningite position. His defence of Lord John Russell's motion for a Bill to enable Manchester, Leeds, and Birmingham to return members to Parliament is significant: 'The government and legislature must keep pace with the spirit of the age. They should neither be behind it, nor before it.'[3] He believed that the middle classes should have more adequate representation. Their national importance gave them a legitimate claim on more political power. He continued to speak with the moderation of a Canningite, but his attitude on representation was more liberal than that of his former leader.

Yet Huskisson still maintained that he was an enemy 'to what is called parliamentary reform on principle; that is, to any general reform in the formation of the House of

1 Parker, C. S., *Life and Letters of Sir James Graham*, i. 86 (2 vols. London, 1907).

2 Stapleton, A. G., *George Canning and His Times*, 344 (London, 1859).

3 *Speeches*, iii. 495.

Commons, which is founded upon the principle of theoretical improvement.'[1] 'I take my stand', he declared, 'upon the aggregate excellence of our representative system and I leave to others to take what delight they may in hunting out the anomalies of its detail.'[2] Security against the dangers of theoretical reform and revolutionary change could best be attained through the representation of the great industrial centres. The claim that the large cities, under the existing system possessed virtual representation was in Huskisson's opinion mere sophistry: 'If great and influential interests have silently grown up in the country, mixing private speculations with large public results, the principle of virtual representation becomes inapplicable to their immediate condition.'[3] In this, as in other aspects of his political thinking, Huskisson evolved policy from existing facts. To make constitutional adjustments in accordance with social developments, to change because of a social pressure for change was the essence of his statesmanship. It was a statesmanship that could find an easy and welcome place in even the most advanced political party of the day. Grey's ministry might have been too Whiggish. Peel's might have been too Conservative. A new Liberal party embracing the Canningites and the younger Whigs would probably have been the most adequate medium for realizing his ideas, and towards this Huskisson looked. The tragic accident at the opening of the Liverpool and Manchester railway in September 1830, when Huskisson was killed by a locomotive, prevented the fashioning of such new party alinements. Hence the Canningites came from the wilderness to a resting place in the fold of the Whigs. 'The Canning Faction has lost its cornerstone' was Creevey's comment on hearing of Huskisson's death. It was too true. His followers such as Palmerston and Lamb had no alternative but to move into the Whig ranks; and a party which, if later reinforced, might have adumbrated much of Gladstonian Liberalism died with Huskisson.

The most cursory survey of Huskisson's political career and an examination of the nature of parties at the time

[1] *Speeches*, iii. 491. [2] *Ibid.* 424. [3] *Ibid.* 433.

reveal forcibly how party alinements had thwarted his talents and hampered to a large degree his reforming ideas. His accomplishments do not bear an accurate ratio to his powers, and his political grouping was in part responsible. His association with Canning, inevitable under the circumstances, proved a handicap. Loyalty to this brilliant man, who moved in the traditions of Pitt, kept Huskisson out of office from 1809 to 1814; robbed him of the Chancellorship of the Exchequer in 1812, and in 1814 reduced him to the obscure Commissionership of Woods and Forests. Under parliamentary institutions, unless a man moves in a strong party, his potentiality for accomplishment seldom finds expression. If he is unfortunate in his political associations, he may, like a rider in a race, be pocketed or jostled out to the fringe of the course, where natural power will avail little. Such was the case with Huskisson. The political connexions which he early made and his advanced ideas on politico-economic problems constitute the chief reasons why he remained for many years in Parliament little more than an advocate, arguing briefs on which favourable judgements were not placed. Only during the short period 1822–27 did party formations bring to him the office which provided ample scope for his constructive ideas. Fortunately within this brief period he performed work which justifies his place among the reformers of the century.

Other factors in addition to his political grouping undoubtedly tended to minimize Huskisson's successes. His oratory was not of the kind that made an appeal in a period when brilliant declamation more often won triumphs than sober, luminous speaking. In his later years, as Greville reminds us, he was 'listened to with attention upon any subject', because of the clarifying light which he invariably threw upon it. But he would earlier have attained parliamentary prestige had he possessed something of Canning's magic brilliance. More serious was the fact that his personality lacked warmth, and his judgement in dealing with other politicians was often gravely in error. His relations with Wellington provide instances of his lack of tact. The most notable of these was his hasty and badly worded note to Wellington offering resignation after he had voted against the Government on the questions raised in connexion with Penryn and East Retford. As most contemporaries observed, a tactful man would have waited at least a day and would have consulted Wellington in person. Greville none too strongly described him as acting 'with the greatest imprudence'.[1] Lord Ellenborough, a shrewd member of Wellington's Government, remarked that Huskisson 'was an able man, but he would never do as a member of a Cabinet in which he was not chief'. He lacked the subtle little ingenuities that constitute in the personal relationships of politics the part of lubricants, necessary for success in a parliamentary system.

Such then in broad outline is the political background to the economic questions which ominously pressed upon Great Britain in the post-war period and absorbed the energies of Huskisson and his fellow-reformers. The long period of war synchronizing with the industrialization of Britain and the expansion of British trade had created new and intricate problems. The party platforms of the eighteenth century had now little to suggest; had few guides to statesmen in dealing with the society of the new century. Early Liberalism associated with the names of Canning and Huskisson was therefore developed in an effort to outline a policy that would enable the state to provide for the new needs. In the succeeding chapters an attempt will be made to illustrate the nature of nascent nineteenth-century Liberalism in its attack on some of the leading problems confronting Great Britain between 1815–30. The one unifying thread in the reforms of the period is the assault on mercantilism, and with this view in mind, Huskisson's accomplishments in economic policy will be described.

[1] Greville's *Journal*, i, 398 (2 vols. New York, 1875).

II

THE CURRENCY PROBLEM

IN the period covered by Huskisson's political career three vital economic problems emerged to challenge the resources of British statesmanship: (i) There was the long-drawn controversy over currency which arose out of the monetary disturbances of the war, and continued long after Waterloo to be a disturbing factor in the period of peace. Seldom in Great Britain's history was the problem of currency so critical, for her strength in the war and her ready recovery and development after it depended on the careful handling of the public credit. (ii) There was agricultural ferment. Largely as a consequence of the war and the rapid growth of the industrial population, a great extension of cultivation had taken place, rents had risen, corn prices fluctuated rapidly, and the agriculturists were sensitively determined to maintain and to advance their interests under the new industrial régime. Hence during the thirty years after the Peace of 1815 the interests and grievances of agriculturists held the stage in political life. (iii) There was a marked industrial expansion which necessitated the discovery of new markets. It is with the last of these questions, the extension of British commerce through the removal of fiscal and navigation restraints, that the name of Huskisson is usually associated. But in the settlement of all these problems his influence was felt, and in the present chapter his association with the currency question must be briefly treated.

The controversy over currency was an occasion for a pitched battle between the mercantilism of the period and the newer political economy of Smith and Ricardo with which the Liberalism of Huskisson was closely wedded. It was the first important issue which brought out distinctly how much of the new economic science Huskisson had absorbed and how ably he championed its principles. It was the earliest of those formidable problems that he tackled. The salient facts of the controversy are readily told. The obvious starting-point is the suspension of cash payments in 1797 by the Bank of England, acting under the authority of an order in council issued by Pitt's Government. The immediate cause of such action was the shrinkage in the amount of cash in the Bank, due partly to the requirements of the Government and partly to excessive demands from the public consequent upon rumours of foreign invasion. Another fact had probably some influence. In 1796 France returned from assignats to a metallic currency and there developed in England a tendency to export gold to a country in which the demand was strong.[1] Many of the smaller country banks, unable to withstand the drain of specie, became bankrupt, and a public panic ensued. By the end of 1796 the Bank's position was extremely precarious. The supply of coin and bullion was reduced to 2½ millions, while the liabilities were 16½ millions. In February 1797 the cash in the Bank dropped to 1½ millions. The Cabinet afraid that the Bank would be unable 'to answer the exigencies of the public service' took immediate action. After a special meeting of the Privy Council, a minute was dispatched to the Bank, asking it to suspend further cash payments. It was generally presumed that this measure was an expedient due to a financial emergency and intended merely to tide over the exigencies of that particular year. Indeed the Act to confirm the order in council was to continue for approximately only seven weeks.[2] But both the Bank and the Government continued to find it so convenient in relieving their difficulties that by frequent renewals it was maintained for twenty-two years.

The immediate effects of the suspension upon the currency were not appreciable. But from 1800 there were signs of inflation, and from that year warning voices were raised. Boyd wrote to Pitt in 1801 that the note issue was excessive, and attributed the fall in the exchanges and the

[1] Hawtrey, R. G., 'The Bank Restriction of 1797' (*Economic Journal*, xxviii. 58).

[2] Andreades, A., *History of the Bank of England*, 201 (London, 1909).

rise in the price of provisions to the redundancy of paper.[1] Sir Francis Baring, Henry Thornton, and Francis Horner expressed similar views. In 1803 Lord King in the House of Lords voiced the opinion that there had been an excess issue of paper.[2] Up to 1808, however, such arguments lacked weight owing to the fact that the suspension caused no very acute financial disturbances. But in 1808 and the subsequent year two phenomena became pronounced: a fall in foreign exchange, and a rise in the price of bullion in terms of the existing currency. Ricardo's acute mind investigated both facts, and in the autumn of 1809 appeared his three famous letters to the *Morning Chronicle*, in which he attributed both phenomena to an excess of inconvertible paper.[3] In lucid and forcible arguments he exposed the prevailing misconceptions on the subject and showed that a depreciation of the currency had taken place due to the suspension of cash payments and the consequent over-issue of paper money. The proofs of such depreciation were found in the two facts mentioned: the low rate of the foreign exchange and the high price of bullion in terms of the existing currency. Gold had risen from the mint price of £3 17*s*. 10½*d*. to as much as £4 13*s*., an advance of almost 20 per cent., which represented a corresponding depreciation in Bank notes. The kernel of Ricardo's argument is that the gold would not have risen, had the notes been convertible, for the Bank would not have been tempted to over-issue. He pointed with warning finger to the evils of such depreciation, and, while not demanding an immediate resumption of cash payments, strongly recommended a limitation in the amount of Bank paper.

In the next year Ricardo followed up his letters by a pamphlet in which he covered more fully the same ground. His arguments had the desired effect of raising the subject

1 Boyd, W., *A Letter to the Right Hon. W. Pitt on the Influence of the Stoppage of Issues in Specie* (London, 1801).

2 *Parliamentary Debates* i, 1836.

3 Ricardo's letters appeared in the issues of 29 August, 20 September, 23 November.

into a position of first importance, and in 1810 the currency question was introduced to Parliament by 'that genuine but sober lover of freedom', Francis Horner. In Horner, a Whig of the new school steeped in the political economy of the time, Ricardo's ideas had a staunch defender. On 1 February he moved for accounts and returns respecting the existing state of the circulating medium and for a committee to consider the subject. On the 19th of the same month the committee was appointed 'to inquire into the cause of the high price of gold bullion and to take into consideration the state of the circulating medium and of the exchange between Great Britian and foreign parts'. Its prominent members were: Francis Horner (the Chairman), William Huskisson (who occupied the Chair in Horner's absence), Sir Henry Parnell, an Irish economist, Spencer Perceval, Chancellor of the Exchequer, R. B. Sheridan, Henry Thornton, and Tierney. The committee held sittings to 25 May, having examined twenty-nine witnesses. By early autumn its report, which became a landmark in the currency history of the nineteenth century, was in the hands of the public.[1]

The main arguments and conclusions of the Bullion Committee are so well known as to require only brief reference. In the opening of their report they drew attention to the financial phenomena of the preceding years, the high price of gold and the lowness of the foreign exchange. The market price of gold was about 15 per cent. above the mint price. In the matter of foreign exchange, Hamburgh, Amsterdam, and Paris, the three principal places with which exchanges were then established, respectively showed rates against Britain at £9 per cent. below par, £7 per cent. below par, and £14 per cent. below par. Following closely in the steps of Ricardo they concluded that such conditions were due to the depreciation of the domestic currency, notwithstanding the popular opinion amongst bankers that the price of gold was due to its scarcity and to the continental demand. Gold bullion was

[1] Hansard, 17, Part viii, p. cci, or see reprint of the report in Cannan, E., *The Paper Pound of 1797–1821* (London, 1919).

neither scarce nor dear, either in England or on the continent, for its value in relation to commodities had not risen. In England gold was easily procurable, granted that the necessary price was paid. Similarly the committee rejected the opinion that the unfavourableness of the foreign exchange was due to an alleged excess of imports over exports. In fact, during the preceding years, the exports exceeded the imports, conclusive proof that the mercantile balance of trade theory was of little value in explaining the movement of the exchange. The soundest explanation for the unfavourable foreign exchange was the same as that for the high price of bullion, a depreciation in the currency consequent upon an excess issue of bank notes. The evidence of a few merchants, including N. M. Rothschild, confirmed the committee in their conclusion that bullion was 'the true regulator both of the value of the currency and of the rate of foreign exchanges; and that the free convertibility of paper currency into the precious metals, and the free exportation of those metals, place a limit to the fall of the exchange, and not only check the exchanges from falling below that limit, but recover them by restoring the balance.'[1]

The committee saw little difficulty in demonstrating the existence of an excessive issue of paper. The confession of the governor of the Bank was almost in itself sufficient proof. He admitted that in their issues no attention whatever had been paid to the price of bullion and to the foreign exchange. Nor had they thought that such attention was necessary. The Bank had been assured that in confining its discount of mercantile bills 'to paper of undoubted solidity, arising out of real commercial transactions and payable at short and fixed periods', it was avoiding any danger of over-issue. The committee rejected the governor's explanation that such an arrangement was an adequate guarantee against an excessive issue. They drew attention to the distinction between an advance of capital to merchants and an increased supply of currency to the general mass of the circulating medium, and pointed out

[1] Cannan, 21.

that in the existing circumstances advances to merchants constituted additions to the currency: 'Each successive advance repeats the same process—if the amount of discounts is progressively increasing, the amount of paper which remains out in circulation over and above what is wanted for the occasions of the public will progressively increase also; and the money prices of commodities will progressively rise.' [1] They claimed that the true tests of over-issue and depreciation were the price of bullion and the condition of the foreign exchanges. The neglect of such tests had resulted in the silent inflation of bank notes with the attendant evils which the committee briefly enumerated: an increase of price in all monetary transactions for time, injury to public and private annuitants and creditors, an unintended advantage gained by the Government and other debtors, inconvenience in the payment of certain classes of public servants whose pay, if once raised, in consequence of a depreciated currency, cannot be conveniently reduced, and finally the temptation to resort to a permanent depreciation of gold coin by an alteration of the standard.

The committee were not content with a diagnosis. They suggested as the sole remedy that the circulating medium be brought back to the principle of cash payments at the option of the holders of notes. The Bank should be allowed freedom in prescribing the mode of effecting the resumption, but the time for the resumption should be definitely fixed at two years, whether or not the war continued. Also the committee pointed out a serious mistake in legally limiting by the usury law the rate of discount to 5 per cent. A higher rate should be allowed, for a high rate was a deterrent on trade borrowing.

The committee's conclusions came to bankers and merchants like a thunderbolt. The prospect of any tinkering with the currency violently disturbed a war-strained public, and deflation was dreaded as a thing of evil. A number of mercantile houses in London failed. Others were brought to the brink of collapse. A controversy began on the merits of the report, and sharp criticism was passed

[1] Cannan, 51.

upon the leading members of the committee. Even the honesty of their motives was questioned. The doctrines of Horner, the Chairman, 'were deemed theoretical and visionary and his conduct impracticable, hazardous to the country, and ruinous to himself'. [1] Huskisson wrote that 'several of those who have taken upon themselves to controvert the report have gone out of their way to misrepresent the conduct, and to cast obloquy on the characters and motives of those who concurred in it'.[2] There was a general opinion that the report was contrary to the evidence heard. Certain economic writers denied emphatically that it was convincing in attributing the financial disturbances to an over-issue of paper. It was claimed that instead of an excessive and hence depreciated paper, the quantity of gold in the country owing to Britain's war operations was scarce. In other words, gold had appreciated. The stream of comment and criticism continued for many years. The question of the currency bulked so large in public attention that the report continued to be subjected to the most severe analysis. In 1822 Joseph Lowe complained that 'in historical and commercial matter, the report is very defective; no notice is taken in it of the pecuniary embarrassments of 1795 and 1796, arising from the double drain of specie for subsidies and corn; nor is the recurrence of these causes in 1799 and 1809 adverted to, although it was to them that we owed the chief increase of our bank notes'. [3] He suggested that the committee did not keep close enough to facts, and was not sufficiently mindful that the suspension of cash payments was coincident with a period of war and acute economic transition, and that other factors besides paper currency influenced Britain's financial situation. Thomas Tooke, writing in 1838, brought the effects of the restriction under a microscopic examination, and considered that the

[1] Lord Holland, *Further Memoirs of the Whig Party*, 103 (London, 1905).

[2] *Speeches*, i. 'The Question Concerning the Depreciation of the Currency', 51.

[3] Lowe, J., *Present State of England*, pt. ii., App. ch. 3. 30 (London, 1822).

committee exaggerated its influence on war prices and the exchanges. The fluctuation of prices on the continent was quite as pronounced as in England, and as in the case of England was due to the exceptional conditions of the war. The committee attributed to the restriction phenomena which in all probability would have appeared without it. For example, the divergence between paper and gold instead of being due to an excess of paper was in large part due to the acute demand for gold abroad in payment of war subsidies: 'In the divergence between the paper and the gold, it was the gold that by increased demand departed from the paper, and not the paper by increased quantity from the gold.'[1] The strongest evidence that Tooke adduced in favour of this view was that the exchanges invariably improved whenever expenditure in gold diminished abroad. When the payment in subsidies had entirely ceased, the exchanges and the price of gold were restored to par, notwithstanding that the Bank circulated more notes than at any preceding period. Tooke was undoubtedly right. He did not take up the cudgels for the Bank. He agreed emphatically with the committee in their condemnation of the manner in which the Bank directors regulated the issue, but he drew attention soundly to some of the subtleties of the situation overlooked by Huskisson and his fellow-investigators.

Moreover, the recommendation of the committee that resumption should take place in two years was under the circumstances hardly wise. While the currency remained depreciated such action would have damaged credit. Ricardo, in September 1821, was careful to admit this in a letter to Wheatley:

'I never should advise a government to restore a currency which was depreciated 30 per cent. to par. . . It was without any legislation that the currency from 1813 to 1819 became . . . within 5 per cent. of the value of gold,—it was in this state of things, and not with a currency depreciated 30 per cent., that I advised a recurrence to the old standard.'[2]

[1] Tooke, T., *History of Prices*, i. 158 (London, 1838).

[2] Quoted in Andreades, *History of the Bank of England*, xx (preface).

Whatever are the criticisms of the bullion report, it was none the less fruitful as a whole in history, and to Huskisson is due a large part of the credit for its compilation. He, Thornton, and Horner were the three members of the committee who composed it. Its importance consists in the clear statement and soundness of its doctrines rather than in the accuracy of its diagnosis. It erred somewhat in its judgement of the existing situation, but seldom have the fundamental principles of a currency resting on a gold standard been better expounded. Its ideas on the relation of currency to the exchanges were not novel. To go no further back than 1804 they may be found in the report on Irish currency of that year.[1] But the historical and dramatic circumstances surrounding the issue of the report of 1810 combined with its able character gave it far greater importance than the earlier document. Ricardo who defended it against the attacks of Charles Bosanquet, a banker and a governor of the South Sea Company, described it as 'a more just exposition of the true principles which should regulate the currency of nations, than has before appeared in any authoritative shape in this or any other country.'[2] Its principles may now seem to be the commonplaces of economics, but the slightest perusal of debates in the period when it appeared is convincing that they were not then regarded as commonplaces. It disposed of the premises and defences of the old balance of trade theory, and thereby marked the entrance into a parliamentary document of the newer political economy associated with the names of Smith and Ricardo. It staked the way for much future legislation. The Resumption Act of 1819 and Peel's Bank Act of 1844 followed largely the lines of its suggestions. Even to-day, when currency theories are in the melting-pot, defenders of a gold standard may find their arguments ably and eloquently presented in the bullion report.

After the violent criticism of the report, Huskisson's

[1] For a good summary of this report, see Macleod, H. D., *Theory of Credit*, ii, pt. ii. 845 (2 vols. London, 1893).

[2] Gonner, E. C., *Economic Essays by Ricardo*, 63 (London, 1923).

friends urged him to defend the views for which he was responsible as a leading member of the committee. In October 1810 he did so in a pamphlet which answered much of the contemporary criticism.[1] His statements were not merely a defence of the report but an acute and extended exposition of its arguments. He illustrated the need of the precious metals as a standard of value for a circulating medium, indicated how the condition of a currency affected foreign exchanges and trade, pressed home the conclusion that a paper currency must be convertible into the precious metals, and described how the resumption might best be effected. But in view of Huskisson's later part in the movement of fiscal and commercial reform, the most interesting portion of his pamphlet was his attack upon the sheet-anchor of contemporary mercantilism, the balance of trade theory. Three opinions were prevalently accepted at the time: (i) Whenever the exchange was against a country, the natural and general course of balancing the account was by a payment of bullion. (ii) The balance of these payments in favour of a country was finally to be measured by the balance of trade, that is by the excess of exports over imports. (iii) The balance of payments might for a time be much against a country, although the balance of trade might be in its favour. Huskisson sought to upset these generalizations by demonstrating that the first, on which the others rested, was not true. Bullion did not generally enter into mercantile operations, and there was no need for it to do so since trade was finally an exchange of equivalents. An unfavourable course of exchange operated as a bounty upon all exports and as a tax upon imports 'by the joint effect of which in all ordinary cases, without any transmission of bullion, the real exchange is brought back to its par, and probably rises above it'.[2] He repudiated the old cherished fallacy of expecting an increase of wealth from an excess of exports over imports. The excess is not 'the measure and realization of the profit derived to us from our foreign trade, but is in fact only capital sent out

[1] *Speeches*, i, pp. 50 ff.

[2] *Ibid.* 96.

of the country for which no capital is returned to it'. Much of the excess consisted in expenditure on armies and fleets abroad and on subsidies to foreign states. Such payments, however politically desirable, could not increase the wealth of the state. From these premises Huskisson moved to the essential basis of the free trade doctrine:

'Commerce enables the population of each separate district to make the most of its peculiar advantages, whether derived from nature, or acquired by the application of industry, talent and capital—to make the most of them for its own consumption; leaving at the same time, the greatest possible remainder to be given in exchange for any other commodities produced more easily, more abundantly, or of better quality, in other districts of the world.' [1]

Huskisson's investigation of currency problems led him into the wider subject of international trade and exchange, and his pamphlet of 1810 foreshadowed the Huskisson of the twenties who made the first substantial breaches in Great Britain's fiscal and commercial system. The overthrow of British mercantilism only came when the new political economy had penetrated the thought of statesmen. The leaven was early noticeable in Huskisson. The economics of Smith and Ricardo provided him with the germinal ideas of his policy, and the currency controversy is the first issue which establishes the fact.

In 1811 the bullion report came under parliamentary criticism. 'Scarcely any subject', stated the *Annual Register*, 'occupied more of the attention of the House of Commons during this session than the consideration of the report of the committee, appointed in the preceding session, to examine and report on the bullion and currency of the kingdom.' On 6 May Horner moved the House into committee and introduced sixteen resolutions embodying the essential ideas of the bullionists.[2] He was aided by Huskisson, Thornton, and with certain qualifications by Canning. But his resolutions were negatived, and on 13 May Vansittart brought forward his rival resolutions supported by the ministry. Two of the most important were seven and fifteen. Seven stated 'that the unfavourable state of the

1 *Ibid.* 103.

2 Hansard, 19. 830.

exchanges and the high price of bullion, do not appear to have been produced by the restriction upon cash payments at the Bank of England or by any excess in the issue of bank notes'. Fifteen provided the explanation 'that the situation of this Kingdom in respect of its political and commercial relations with foreign countries . . . is sufficient without any change in the internal value of its currency to account for the unfavourable state of the foreign exchanges and for the high price of bullion'. These resolutions, as has been pointed out, contained considerable truth. Apart from the restriction there were other causes of the lowness of the foreign exchanges. But Vansittart was not so fortunate in all his statements, particularly in the third resolution in which he claimed that bank notes 'have hitherto been, and are at this time, held in public estimation to be equivalent to the legal coin of the realm', and flatly denied any depreciation. Such a resolution flew in the face of all the evidence, and rightly aroused Canning to a strong assault on the position of the bullionists. 'I cannot', declared he, 'believe it possible until the vote shall actually have passed, that any assembly of reasonable men can be persuaded to give their concurrence.' But Vansittart's arguments, including the extravagant claim that the restriction had supplied the country with the resources for the war, persuaded the House of Commons, and the existing arrangements were to be maintained until after the conclusion of peace. Huskisson and his colleagues were forced to await a later occasion for the triumph of their position.

It is needless to describe the events immediately subsequent to the debate on the bullion report. It is well known how Lord King was determined to disprove the claim of Vansittart that the promissory notes of the Bank were equivalent to the legal coin of the realm by requiring his tenants to pay their rents in either gold or notes sufficient to purchase an equal weight of standard gold at the market price of the day.[1] His action was exceedingly embarrassing to the Government, for it brought out effectively the

[1] See his circular to his tenants, Hansard, 20. 792–3.

differences between payments in paper and in coin, differences of which the minister had wished to deny the existence. The Government's hand was forced, and it carried an Act forbidding all differences between payments in paper and in coin, or virtually making bank notes legal tender. So the matter remained for the time being, but throughout the succeeding years the stormy Cobbett thundered in his *Register* on the evils of paper currency, and succeeded in keeping the subject before public attention. The financial and commercial depression after 1815 made opinion favourable to a renewed discussion of the question, and in 1818–19 the controversy once more blazed into life. Huskisson's pamphlet was reprinted and read greedily for the bullionist case. Discussion became as fervid and popular as in 1810–11. It inspired Sydney Smith with the remark that in town he obtained nothing at table but soup and bullion.

On 2 February 1819 Tierney introduced the subject to Parliament by a resolution for an inquiry into the effects of the restriction on the exchanges and the state of the circulating medium. Vansittart, still Chancellor of the Exchequer, favoured discussion of the subject, and secret committees were appointed by the House of Lords and the House of Commons. Peel was Chairman of the latter on which also sat Castlereagh, Vansittart, Canning, Tierney, and Huskisson. The committee introduced two reports. The first recommended the strict expediency of returning to cash payments, but recognized that the Bank would require a considerable amount of cash on hand. Hence it recommended that such payments in gold as the Bank had been voluntarily making since 1816 should stop. Most of the gold so paid had been drawn away to France. The second report laid down as a primary condition for the resumption the repayment of a large portion of the debt due by the public to the Bank, and outlined the manner in which the resumption should take place. On 24 May Peel in a luminous speech introduced resolutions on the reports.[1] Surrendering to the logic of his own mind, he

[1] Hansard, 40. 675–705.

confessed that although he had formerly opposed the conclusions of the Bullion Committee, he now accepted them and pressed their acceptance upon the House. He wrote characteristically to a friend:

'I have read the bullion report of 1810 with the utmost attention—with the same attention with which I would read the proof of a proposition in mathematics. I can find no defect in the argument, and therefore I am bound to come to the conclusion that paper was depreciated, and that the high price of bullion and the low rate of exchange were the criteria by which to judge the extent of that depreciation.'[1]

Peel's resolutions were carried, and a Bill was passed to the effect that 'after 1 May 1823 cash payment of notes, on demand in the legal coin of the realm should be resumed; and that previous to that date, payment of notes could be demanded in bullion only at a successively reduced rate'. Thus took place what an historian considered 'the most important incident in the financial history of the present century.'[2] Cobbett's 'colossus of tyranny and fraud' collapsed. The proposals of Huskisson and his fellow Liberals of 1810 were vindicated, and a tantalizing cause of financial fluctuation was removed. But it cannot be assumed that Parliament's sanction to the resumption of cash payments in 1819 was a covert criticism of the refusal of Parliament in 1811 to accept the resolutions of the Bullion Committee. In 1819 the paper was only slightly depreciated—within 5 per cent. of its par value—and resumption being rendered easier was therefore far more defensible than it would have been in 1810 or 1813.

The resumption was not without ill consequences. Deflation generally brings in its train as many evils as inflation, although in this particular instance the evils were probably not great. None the less, the restriction, while in operation, had created its own vested interests which were now in danger. Many individuals suffered or claimed

[1] Parker, C. S., *Sir Robert Peel and His Private Papers*, i. 293 (3 vols. London, 1899).

[2] Walpole, Spencer, *History of England from the Conclusion of the Great War*, i. 406 (2 vols. London, 1907).

to suffer from the resumption. In particular the agriculturists were stricken with a sense of grievance. Early in 1822, under the leadership of Western, they collected forces for a grand assault upon Peel's Act, and enlisted as an ally the erratic Cobbett, whose vast exaggerations were sufficient to damn any cause. He endeavoured to convince the popular mind that the fall in agricultural prices had nothing in the least to do with the character of the seasons or with a glut in the corn market, but was wholly due to a change in the volume of money. Worthy of more attention were the arguments of Western.[1] He was not modest in his claims, for he argued that all the financial and business difficulties of the country must be wholly attributed to the resumption: 'This was the irresistible source of the general suffering. It pressed on every branch of industry; it affected every class of community; it contracted every tendency to national improvement or prosperity.'[2] The agriculturists, he claimed, suffered in many ways. He attributed the low price of wheat, so injurious to farmers and landlords, to a scarcity of the currency consequent upon the resumption of cash payments. Upon the same measures, but more inexplicably, he placed the blame for the heavy taxation of the agriculturists which aggravated their financial worries. He pleaded not merely the distresses of the class whom he represented but endeavoured to show, as others have shown under similar circumstances, how those who entered into contracts during the suspension of cash payments now lost under the resumption. Most of the existing pecuniary contracts were of course entered into since 1797. His illustrations were adequate enough to bring out the salient points that he wished to prove, but far too exaggerated to apply in the actual circumstances of the time. For example, he argued that raising the value of money one-half through resumption might deprive some men of their entire income. But the resumption of 1819 did not raise the value of the currency one-half, and although there was some pecuniary loss, the great evil which Western described was largely a myth.

[1] Hansard, 2nd ser., 7. 877.

[2] *Ibid.* 878.

His solution for the existing distress was the substitution of a system which would give to the products of industry of every description the same relative money price which they commanded during the suspension of cash payments. His suggestion was not unlike that of many European economists and statesmen after the Great War, 1914–18, devaluation; stabilizing the value of the currency at approximately its existing value under the depreciation. Such an arrangement would save business and those who had monetary transactions from the distresses of deflation.

Huskisson, as one of the strongest champions in Parliament of a return to cash payments, had the chief task of answering Western. He did so in one of his ablest speeches.[1] A contemporary wrote of it as uniting 'correct reasoning with clear, elegant, and forcible expression, in a degree rarely met with in the discussions of abstract topics',[2] and a later historian described it in a burst of admiration as 'one of the most remarkable financial addresses ever delivered in the House of Commons'.[3] Apart from all exaggerations there is no doubt concerning the ability of the speech. The fact is that Huskisson had little difficulty in crushing some of Western's rickety ideas on the subject of currency, but he was perhaps not wholly just to the latter's devaluation proposal. Nowadays there would be many who would be ready to support Western's idea of stabilizing a depreciated currency, and who would remain unconvinced by Huskisson's powerful speech. Indeed a body of European statesmen blessed the general principle of devaluation in the Conference of Genoa in April 1922. The one difficulty with Western's suggestion is that the currency was hardly depreciated enough to warrant devaluation. Under the circumstances it would make little difference to business whether the currency was deflated or devaluated. But Huskisson took Western's suggestions very seriously. To Western's plea that adjustments be made to save from any loss those who made contracts during the suspension, he replied reasonably

[1] *Speeches*, ii. 129. [2] *Annual Register*, 1822.

[3] Walpole, Spencer, *History of England*, ii. 110.

enough that adjustments between debtors and creditors to be equitable must embrace contracts prior as well as subsequent to 1797, and that would be impracticable. Upon Western's plan of devaluating the currency, Huskisson poured scorn. He declared that such a thing would be a 'death-blow to all public credit, and to all confidence in private dealings between man and man. Does he not see that if you once lower your standard, it will become a precedent that will be resorted to on every future emergency or temporary pressure—resorted to the more readily, as credit and every other valuable resource, on which this country has hitherto relied, will be at an end?'[1] There is considerable weight in his remarks, but he follows them up with others unnecessarily alarming. It was extravagance to claim that if Western's plan were acted upon it would bring 'strife, insolvency, stagnation of business, individual misery, and general disorder'. On the contrary a very reasonable case could be made out for the general principle of devaluation. Huskisson, however, must be pardoned for a certain extravagance and unfairness in his defence of resumption. He looked upon it as a measure of statesmanship essential to insure stability in a country wracked by fluctuating prices and general commercial depression, and it seemed to be endangered by the attacks of the agriculturists. Hence the vigour with which he repudiated the arguments of its assailants.

With no less trenchancy he dealt with Western's suggestion that wheat instead of gold be made the standard of value, on the principle that 'the standard of value in every country should be that article which forms the constant and most general food of its population'. It was easy for him to show the difficulties in this suggestion. In Ireland potatoes would be the standard, and transactions between the two countries could scarcely be facilitated by the maintenance of a wheat standard for the one and a potato standard for the other. Furthermore, such a standard would lack stability, for it would fluctuate with the variations in the price of wheat. A little obscurity in Western's remarks

1 *Speeches*, ii. 144.

led Huskisson to argue that what Western really meant was not that wheat should be either money or standard, but that the standard of money instead of being fixed once for all should be varied from time to time according to the price of wheat. This arrangement would cause such fluctuations that 'the wit of man . . . could not devise a scheme better adapted to destroy all confidence and credit'. He concluded his speech with a reference to the great currency controversy in the reign of William III, which showed a situation parallel to that existing at the time. Up to 1696 the currency had been depreciated. In that year it was restored, with the consequence that the country suffered from much the same difficulties as in the years after 1819. In the face of a popular demand for the restoration of the clipt money, Parliament adopted the proposal of Montague, 'That this House will not alter the Standard of the Gold and Silver Coins of this Kingdom in fineness, weight, or denomination'. With telling effect Huskisson shrewdly proposed to amend Western's motion for an examination of the resumption by moving the famous resolution of 1696. The debate was continued on the succeeding day, when Western's motion was defeated by 194 to 30. Huskisson's amendment in the form of Montague's resolution was carried. The debate had been vivid, and had drawn in the leading parliamentarians. Ricardo, Peel, and the Marquis of Londonderry were Huskisson's weightiest supporters, while Brougham and Attwood, who might be described as the chief currency crank of the period, supported Western.

This was by no means the last occasion when the resumption of cash payments was under critical discussion. Western's ardour for a change in the existing system was unquenchable. Supported by Attwood he many times came back to the attack. On 10 July of the same year he re-opened the question with eighteen lengthy resolutions which were negatived.[1] On 12 June 1823 he again moved for a committee on the state of the currency. In this year he and those of his opinion pleaded that at least there

[1] Hansard, 2nd ser., 7. 1596.

should be equitable adjustment of contracts for those who had suffered from the resumption. Once more Huskisson was a staunch defender of Peel's Act, and readily exposed the fallacy of the equitable adjustment argument. If the principle was to be acted upon 'it would be necessary to have more courts of chancery throughout the kingdom than public-houses; and even then it would be impossible to dispose of all the cases in thirty years'.[1] Thus, like Peel in the same debate, he disposed of equitable adjustments as utterly impracticable.

It is only justice to Western and to the agriculturists to point out that although they greatly exaggerated conditions, there is no doubt that in the period during the resumption of cash payments the lot of the labourer, the farmer, and the landowner was unfortunate in the extreme. The distress amongst these classes was pronounced, and recognized by all who knew anything concerning the country. Prices and nominal wages were tumbling rapidly. A general slump prevailed in markets. Wages sank some 20 per cent. in 1819 and 1820, 12 per cent. more in 1821, and 5 per cent. in 1822.[2] The index numbers of Jevons show clearly the drop in prices. Those farmers who had heavily mortgaged their land in the previous years might well dread the drop in prices. Where Western and his fellow agriculturists erred was not so much in their description of the distress as in their diagnosis of the trouble. They attributed the drop in prices to the contraction of currency due to the resumption of cash payments. There is little doubt that it was partly due to the contraction of the currency, but the contraction was not the result of the resumption. As Macleod has pointed out the decrease in the amount of the currency was caused by the failure of about 300 country banks in 1815–16, and the destruction of about £12,000,000 of their worthless paper.[3] This event was both evil and good. It was good in that it brought the bank note to almost its par value, and hence

[1] *Speeches*, ii. 217.
[2] Porter, G. R., *Progress of the Nation*, 48 (London, 1912).
[3] Macleod, H. D., *Theory of Credit*, ii. 803 (London, 1893).

facilitated resumption, but it necessarily had a depressing effect on prices. But there were other factors contributing to the distress, apart altogether from the currency. Great Britain, after the turmoil of war, was rapidly passing through a period of economic transition, when her industry and her agriculture were both being profoundly changed. As in therapeutics, so in the interpretation of economic phenomena, it is not easy to isolate the causes of a condition. As Huskisson frequently pointed out, the change in the currency was merely one of the disturbing factors in the Britain of the twenties. Its precise importance is difficult to gauge, but at any rate it was only one factor. All the old laws and arrangements concerning economic life, which ill fitted Britain in the post-war period, were as much responsible, and they constituted the imposing problems that confronted Huskisson and the Liberal reformers of the time—the corn laws, the navigation regulations, the prohibitive tariffs, and other enactments which constituted British mercantilism at the opening of the nineteenth century. The first of these problems to require treatment is that of the corn laws. It, as much as the currency, absorbed the thought of Huskisson.

III

THE CORN LAWS

IN the years subsequent to the Napoleonic war British agriculture passed through an era of sharp distress. For over half a century the so-called Agrarian Revolution had been in progress. Changes in agricultural methods were adopted, and enclosures steadily changed the face of the older rural England. The rising prices of farm produce, evident in the last decades of the eighteenth century and pronounced in the war period, resulted in the extension of the enclosure movement and the sinking of capital in the land.[1] A boom in British agriculture set in, and large investments were made in the industry. But with the conclusion of peace in 1814–15 an era of low prices began, and agriculturists were faced by the tantalizing problem of shouldering their capital investments while obtaining for their produce much diminished prices. The burden was accentuated by heavy poor-rates and war taxation. War prices disappeared but war taxes remained, and little wonder that a wail of distress arose from agrarian England. How to escape from the distress was the urgent problem of the period.

The monopoly of the home market seemed to the agriculturists the *sine qua non* of security and prosperity. Their persistent pressure led to the passing of the corn law of 1815. A long struggle ensued to maintain it against the attacks of the industrial classes. The landowners claimed that their interests were those of the nation and that their protection was national protection. Hence the corn law was a refurbished form of mercantilism, pressed upon the state by distressed landowners and struggling farmers. The attitude towards it of Huskisson and early Liberal reformers is of great interest. In the pregnant drama of

1 See Porter, G. R., *Progress of the Nation*, 148, for statistics of prices and enclosures (London, 1851).

economic history that began roughly in 1815 and ended in 1846, Huskisson and the Canningites were prominent actors. Indeed, he and his associates did much to prepare for the final settlement of that thorny issue which so deeply split political forces. On this question as on so many others, he blazed the way for the later statesmanship of Peel.

Something must be said of corn law policy in the past, although it is needless to travel widely in the distant background. Laws change as the motives of public policy change. The corn laws of the seventeenth and eighteenth centuries had a different character and motive from the famous law of 1815. A careful examination of them would lead one into what is as yet a vast and inadequately explored field, where the student of nineteenth-century history in innocent blindness would fall into many dangerous bogholes. In spite of the dangers, some consideration is a necessary prelude to the subject under discussion.

In 1670 the first systematic and comprehensive law imposing duties on the importation of corn was placed on the statute book.[1] It stated that when wheat in the home market was below 53*s.* 4*d.* per quarter, a duty of 16*s.* was imposed; when it was above this price and yet under 80*s.*, an 8*s.* duty; when over 80*s.* the former poundage of 4*d.* was imposed. Other grains had similar graduated rates. The law might seem unmistakably protectionist, and was certainly meant to give encouragement to English agriculture. It was entitled 'An Act for the Improvement of Tillage'. Sir Henry Parnell and advocates of protection in 1813 looked back to it as ideal in the benefit that it conferred on the producer. In 1670 53*s.* 4*d.* for wheat was practically a famine price. Yet the law was not protectionist in the modern sense, for it was not intended to save English agriculturists from a devastating competition. In that period they had no powerful competitors. The country with normal harvests grew enough corn for its needs, and in a time of severe scarcity the import duties were invariably suspended. Whatever may have been the original intention of the duties, they came in time to be considered

[1] 22 Car. II, c. 13.

primarily as supplementary to the bounties paid on export. These bounties appeared in a money grant of 1673, and were systematized by the famous Act of 1689.[1] The import duties tended to correct a common abuse in the bounty system; they prevented corn from being imported for the purpose of re-export with a bounty. For this reason they were maintained throughout the eighteenth century, and gave to nineteenth-century politicians a false impression that they existed solely for the protection of home producers. But in the eighteenth century producers were more interested in the bounties which encouraged export, and it was believed that the bounty system could best attain the prime object of statesmen: 'to prevent grain from being at any time either so dear that the poor cannot subsist or so cheap that the farmer cannot live by growing of it'.[2]

This is not the place to discuss the merits or demerits of the corn bounties. Readers of Adam Smith will recall that he gave them rough handling, which, however, they survived for thirty-eight years, not expiring till 1814. But neither bounties nor import duties remained throughout the eighteenth century as they had been fixed in 1689 and 1670 respectively. In 1773 they were modified considerably.[3] The Act of that year has a singular interest. It won commendation from Adam Smith and later from his nineteenth-century disciple, M'Culloch. Not least, it obtained the praise of Huskisson who in 1827 stated that his object was to restore the corn law to what it was in 1773. An examination of his policy from 1821–7 justifies the statement. According to this statute, wheat, when under 48*s.* a quarter, should pay the former duty of 16*s.*, but when over 48*s.* it was to pay merely a nominal duty of 6*s.* a quarter. New regulations concerning the bounty were also made. The Act was an ingenious attempt to meet the new needs of England for an increased import and at the same time to keep prices steady by relying partly on home-grown and partly on imported corn. But it brought no

[1] 1 William and Mary, c. 12.

[2] Smith, Charles, *Tracts on the Corn Trade and Corn Laws*, 72 (London, 1759).

[3] 13 Geo. III, c. 43.

satisfaction to the landlords, for it seemed to keep prices from rising with an expanding demand.

In the quarter of the century after 1773 an increasing town population necessitated larger supplies of grain, and by 1788 the average annual imports exceeded the exports. The nightmare of low priced foreign grain flooding the British market now disturbed the sleep of British agriculturists. For the next half-century the bogy remained the fertile source of alarm amongst landlords, and largely accounted for the passage of corn laws in 1791, 1804, and 1815.[1] The two former Acts raised the price level at which grain under a nominal duty might enter, and the latter imposed prohibition of import up to a specified price. But the increase of import duties was not merely the product of an excessive greediness of landlords for protection. The price of wheat was rising, and higher duties were necessary to keep pace with the rising price. Moreover, in the parliamentary debate on the Act of 1804 other considerations came before public attention.[2] It was argued that agriculturists were saddled with many burdens, among which the most prominent were the rise in the price of labour and the enhanced poor-rate. Adequate protection would aid the farmer in carrying the extra war-time expenses. A further plea was that amid the exigencies of war a food supply independent of foreign import was imperative. For this purpose more land must be brought into cultivation by enclosing wastes and draining fens, which could only be done by holding out to the agriculturists hopes of adequate protection and high prices. Thus, protective duties emerged largely as a war-time measure to encourage extension of cultivation, but with vested interests silently created the agriculturists clung to the duties as the *sine qua non* of their prosperity and welfare.

Yet the duties in the law of 1804 were practically inoperative. Prices remained well above those at which foreign grain could enter at the nominal duty. In 1813 the price of wheat soared to 109*s.* a quarter. Nevertheless,

[1] 31 Geo. III, c. 30; 44 Geo. III, c. 109; 55 Geo. III, c. 26.

[2] Hansard, 1st ser., (vol.) 2. 478, 481, 784, 939, 957, 1086, 1010.

in this year of high prices, a parliamentary committee complained that the home-grower lacked sufficient protection, and advocated the adoption of a new expedient, prohibition of import until the home price reached a high level. The recommendations of the committee drag us into the corn law controversy that raged with little suspension for the next thirty years, and in which Huskisson from the outset took an active share. The salient facts concerning the committee and its report are easily told.

The committee was proposed on 22 March 1813 with the primary object of examining the Irish corn trade, and indicating a means to encourage it. An amendment extended its investigation to the corn trade of Great Britain. On the committee sat Parnell, Huskisson, Peel, Castlereagh, and Vansittart. The dominant note of its report, ordered to be printed on 11 May 1813, was struck in the opening sentences.[1] It was stated that the value of corn imported into Great Britain during the period 1792–1811 amounted to £58,634,135. The average price of wheat for the same period had been 77*s.* 3*d.* a quarter, and the average price for the last four years 105*s.* 5*d.* 'Your committee are of opinion that so great a degree of dependence on foreign countries for a sufficient supply of food, and so great an advance in the price of wheat as is hereby proved, require the interposition of Parliament without further delay.' Fearful that the foreigner would flood the British market with his produce, the committee in spite of apparent paradox, found the remedy for the two evils of high prices and foreign competition in prohibitive duties. They believed that the British Isles, through an extension of their cultivated lands, could be made completely self-sustaining. The dependence on the foreigner was due to the absence of a restrictive system. The committee suggested remedies. No corn should enter from the continent until the home price rose to 103*s.* When the price was above 103*s.* importation might be allowed with a high duty. Free exportation to all countries should be permissible till wheat rose to 90*s.* 2*d.*

[1] See *British Parliamentary Papers*, Session 1813–14, vol. iii (339).

The report loses weight when we discover the flimsy evidence on which it rested. The committee were satisfied with sending out a set of five questions to the Board of Agriculture and the Farming Society of Ireland, printing the petitions from the millers and corn mill proprietors, and taking evidence at four short sittings from five witnesses. All the information pertained to Ireland. On such meagre data Sir Henry Parnell, chairman of the committee, wished to base resolutions for a new law. He speciously assured the House that the committee had been influenced by no other motive 'than that of a strong sense of the danger of continuing to depend upon our enemies for a sufficient supply of food, and of the impolicy of sending our money to improve other countries while we had so much of our own lands that stood in need of the same kind of improvement'.[1] Notwithstanding this appeal, his resolutions encountered strong opposition, particularly from Lord Archibald Hamilton, Rose, Western, and Francis Horner. Huskisson's remarks are interesting as being his first recorded parliamentary utterances on the corn laws, and from the fact that they were in sharp contrast with his later views. He supported Parnell's resolution, stating that on the committee 'he had been actuated, in his consideration of the important matters referred to it, not by any particular solicitude for the corn growers or the landowners, or for Ireland, in which he had no personal interest; but for the general interests of the whole Empire, which, he was satisfied, would be best consulted by securing to all classes of the community an adequate supply of corn'.[2] Like Parnell, Huskisson believed that British agriculture would receive encouragement from high duties, and would produce an ample food supply for the nation's needs. His ideal for Britain was economic independence, attained through the avenue of high protection. But like other contemporary defenders of a corn law, he was unconscious of its latent evils, and of how ill founded was the belief that protection would promote British agriculture.

The lateness of the session prevented parliamentary

[1] Hansard, 26. 645.

[2] *Speeches*, i. 291.

action, and further discussion was postponed to May 1814. In the interval a confluence of circumstances added new force and interest to the debate. The price of corn, which in 1813 had soared to over 109*s.* a quarter, dropped in 1814 to the average price of 77*s.* 6*d.* The effect of a good harvest, with other subsidiary factors, brought prices down, and gave an excuse for much lamentation on the part of landowners and farmers. It was obvious that Parnell's resolutions would now obtain stronger support, but the opposition also had marshalled its forces. Parnell elaborated his former arguments, moved for free exportation without bounty or duty, stated that the only certain means of a low and stable price for corn was in protective import duties, and drew liberally from Adam Smith in support of his views.[1] He argued that his proposal would reduce the price, because its effect would be 'to promote the growth of corn, by which means a larger supply might be obtained'. His proposed scale of duties was more modest than that in the former year.[2]

Huskisson took a prominent share in the debate. He described the new proposals as having a twofold object to render the country independent of foreign supply and to keep the price of corn as steady as possible.[3] He hopefully and innocently argued that a fluctuating price with dependence on the foreigner could be remedied only by a protective duty. Yet he was inclined to consider Parnell's duties too high. They 'proceeded rather too much upon the principle of giving the monopoly of the English market to the English corn-growers'. In place of Parnell's prohibition of import up to 84*s.*, which tended to give a monopoly to the home producer, he suggested a sliding scale. Sixty-three shillings was to constitute the level at which a prohibitory duty of 24*s.* 3*d.* should operate. As the price rose one shilling, the duty fell proportionably; thus at 86*s.* all duties would be removed. Huskisson

[1] Hansard, 27. 707.

[2] Prohibition of import when home price was below 84*s.*; duty of 2*s.* 6*d.* when price was between 84*s.* and 87*s.*; duty of 6*d.* when price was above 87*s.*

[3] *Speeches*, i. 292.

moved a second amendment that colonial corn should pay a duty only one-half that on foreign corn. Colonial preference was the distinctive note in his legislative proposals. He visualized the Empire as a political unit bound together by material interests, and his championship of colonial preference was his most constructive act in the corn law debate. Parnell accepted the amendments 'for the sake of unanimity'; and Huskisson also had a defender, if a lukewarm one, in Canning who hesitatingly stated that 'he had considerable doubts whether it was necessary or proper to do anything but what had been done; namely, the allowing the free exportation of grain'.[1]

In the ensuing debate the House of Commons became the battleground of self-acclaimed champions of political economy who invoked the teachings of economic science with sacramental ardour. The authority of Adam Smith was claimed on both sides, and his opinions used to prove the most contradictory conclusions. Huskisson, on three occasions, contributed to the argument of the protectionists:

> 'If our other regulations with regard to the price of commodities stood upon the basis of the principles of free trade, then there could be no possible objection to leaving our agricultural productions to find their own level. But, so long as our commerce and manufactures were encouraged and forced by protections, by bounties, and by restraints on importation from abroad, he saw no reason why the laws relating to the growth of corn should alone form an exception to this general system.'[2]

He continued to lay stress on the need of independence from foreign imports and a stable price. But he and Parnell failed to carry a Bill incorporating their resolutions. There was violent opposition to high import duties in the industrial areas. Over one hundred protesting petitions were sent to the Commons, and Vansittart, Chancellor of the Exchequer, bowed before the storm.[3] He moved that the petitions be referred to the consideration of a select com-

[1] Hansard, 27. 955.
[2] *Speeches*, i. 298.
[3] See Smart, W., 'The Antecedents of the Corn Law of 1815' (*English Historical Review*, July 1909, pp. 484 ff.).

mittee. This motion closed the debate for 1814. Although Parnell's major resolutions were rejected, his efforts and those of his supporters were not futile. They had destroyed the 'Carthago delenda est' of Adam Smith, bounties on export. With the bounties went the duties on export. A Bill was carried embodying both provisions, and an old system disappeared with few mourners to bewail its fate.[1]

In February 1815 discussion on the corn laws was resumed. Robinson, Vice-President of the Board of Trade, introduced resolutions covering the chief recommendations of the committee appointed in the previous year. The most important was to the effect that 80*s*. was 'the lowest price which would afford to the British grower an adequate remuneration'. Robinson suggested that the importation of wheat be prohibited altogether when home price was below 80*s*. Such a proposal had no precedent in corn law history, as formerly there had been a graduated scale. Colonial grain might enter when price reached 67*s*. When home price exceeded 80*s*., foreign grain might enter free of duty. The proposals aroused keen debate. From the industrial centres protests against the law streamed to the Commons. 'The greatest number of petitions', remarked Earl Grey, 'that had ever perhaps been known in the history of Parliament.'[2] The Manchester petition echoed the opinions of many in its statement that the Bill would raise the price of labour and handicap manufacturers in their competition with foreigners. Huskisson took active part in the debate, resuming his position of the former year in favour of protection and stating that anything less than 80*s*. 'as a protecting price would not remunerate the farmer'. A Bill embodying Robinson's resolutions was carried in both Houses, and notwithstanding opposition in the towns, the celebrated corn law of 1815 replaced that of 1804.

The Act of 1815 was considered by its staunch supporters as a great measure of public policy beneficial to the nation and the Empire. They repudiated the charge that it was intended simply to advance the interests of

[1] 54 Geo. III, c. 69.

[2] Hansard, 30. 1.

landowners. While paying homage to the abstract principle of free trade, many argued that in the matter of corn, the subsistence of the nation, it could not apply. Among these was Huskisson. Throughout the discussions of 1813–15 he had uniformly stated that the nation should as far as possible be rendered independent of foreign supplies. The agony of the Napoleonic struggle, when the wolf was frequently at the national door, had greatly impressed him. A secure food supply necessitated the protection of agriculture. In the five years succeeding 1815 he maintained this position, and in a speech in May 1820 emphatically reaffirmed it.[1] He put forward two additional arguments in favour of the law of 1815. He pleaded that the protective measures would rightly shelter vested interests. During the years of war agriculture had received artificial protection. Capital was forced into raising corn which would not otherwise have been applied to that object. Vested interests were thus created to satisfy a national need. It seemed only justice when the immediate need was passed to preserve them from violent disturbance. This consideration alone seemed to justify the monopoly of the home market by the home grower until the price of wheat reached 80*s*., but Huskisson's policy comprised more than the provincial interests of Britain. His vision took an imperial sweep. He saw in the corn law an opportunity to confer benefits upon other parts of the Empire, particularly upon Ireland, by encouraging her to produce for the British market: 'To give a superior cultivation to the fertile land of Ireland and to turn British capital into that island must tend to increase, in a very material degree, the resources, and augment the revenue of the Empire.'[2] Was he sound?

Judged from the perspective of a century the statesmanship of the Act of 1815 was faulty. One may ignore the charge that those responsible for the measure were actuated by the selfish interests of landowners and failed to consider national interests. It is not necessary to reject the asseverations of Huskisson and others that they supported the measure because they considered it beneficial

[1] *Speeches*, ii. 45. [2] *Ibid.* 47.

to the nation. Their intention must be attributed to them for grace. It is also unnecessary to dwell on the criticism of the classical economists, like Ricardo, who argued that the poorer lands brought under cultivation during the necessities of war were uneconomic lands, and hence it was neither expedient for their owners nor for consumers that they be retained in grain-growing. In support of this sound argument the law of diminishing returns developed by Malthus, West, and Ricardo was enthusiastically invoked. But a simpler criticism of the corn law was that it lamentably failed to attain its object. The Prime Minister, Lord Liverpool, in defending the Bill stated that 'the important point to attain was a steady and moderate price. . . . The great object was to prevent that fluctuation in the price of the first necessary of life which was so injurious to the consumer'.[1] A glance at average prices in the ten years following 1815 shows how dismally the Act of 1815 disappointed his hopes. Fluctuations in price became more precipitate than they had ever been, and there would have been fluctuations in spite of any corn law. The price of grain varied with the changes in the seasons, and a parliamentary statute was quite incapable of preventing fluctuations. In fact, as will be pointed out, the Act of 1815 accentuated them. It was a very shallow judgement that led Huskisson and his colleagues to assume that it would bring stability in prices.

The corn law failed to satisfy agriculturists and consumers. From 1815 to 1820 the wail of agrarian distress rose from every part of England, and the refrain was ever the same, returns were not adequate to meet expenses. Farmers, accustomed to war prices, had toned their expenditure so high that for many years after the peace they were unable to make the proper adjustment to the low prices. During the high prices of the war the farming class had assumed heavy mortgages to carry out extensive enclosures, and the low prices of the post-war period meant to them virtual disaster. The Act of 1815 had the effect of giving them false and unsubstantial hopes. They

[1] Hansard, 30. 181.

assumed that prices would range round 80*s*.; but on the contrary they were generally much below 80*s*. Thus the corn law became a deceit and a fraud. It raised expectations which in operation it shattered.

In 1817 and 1818 prices exceeded the 80*s*. level, yet agricultural depression remained. 'The present corn laws', stated a writer in the *Edinburgh Review*, 'seem to please nobody . . . the agriculturists whom they were to save from utter ruin, take the lead in seeking their repeal.' In the years 1819–21 some 1,200 petitions were received by the Government from agricultural districts, in which the influx of foreign grain was blamed for the distress. Notwithstanding that the amount of imported corn was slight, the petitioners demanded more adequate protection. They assumed that high duties would bring high prices, and nothing could disabuse them of the idea. But the ministry was adamant in opposition to higher duties. In 1820 Robinson, President of the Board of Trade, reached the conclusion that the cultivation of poor lands was the source of agrarian distress, and declared emphatically that the agriculturists must not expect further protection: 'It was not by any act of the legislature that the land had been called into cultivation, and it was not therefore to be expected that by any act of the legislature it should be continued in cultivation.'[1] Huskisson supported Robinson, and maintained the very doubtful thesis that the law of 1815 was effectual in attaining its purpose. But he was not without sympathy for the agriculturists. As he stated in a letter in January 1820, they will be 'forced to sell a deficient crop at prices which would be barely remunerative, if it had been a most abundant one—it is scarcely to be expected from them, or from any set of men, to reason quite coolly and dispassionately on the cause of their distress'.[2] In the same letter he stated his policy:

'I have always considered a graduated duty as a much wiser and more efficacious regulation than a contingent prohibition, for reasons

[1] Hansard, 2nd ser., I. 643.

[2] Huskisson to Edmund Wodehouse, 20 January 1820. B.M. Add. MS. 38742, f. 3b.

which I stated at the time, and which it would be tedious to detail at present, but at a very full meeting of the landed interest at Fife House, when the option was in their power, the gentlemen present almost unanimously, and particularly Mr. Western, gave a preference to the present Bill; and although I am convinced that it would then have been as easy to pass the one measure as the other, I do not think it safe, if practicable, under all the present circumstances of the country, to attempt to change from the principle which then prevailed, to that which was rejected.'

The Government had also a powerful, if critical, ally in Ricardo who with pitiless logic assailed the demands of the agriculturists.[1] But he was not content with the existing measure, and made the most constructive suggestion of the year in his preference for free trade with a fixed countervailing duty. The *Edinburgh Review*, at that time the standard-bearer of advanced opinions, argued similarly that repeal of the barbarous restraints on corn importation was necessary for the relief of agriculture and the community.

The year 1821 opened with renewed agitation by the agriculturists, and with a fresh stream of petitions. Various were the demands. 'Some', remarked the sober *Annual Register*, 'wished the Government to alter the standard of the currency; some suggested the propriety of expunging part of the national debt; some placed their hopes in the removal of taxes; and some had a perfect faith in the omnipotence of high protecting duties.'[2] Gooch, a spokesman of the discontented interests, pressed for the appointment of a select committee to consider agricultural distress, and this year found the ministry favourable. Notwithstanding the warning voice of Ricardo, fearful of further protection, a committee was appointed. This committee constituted a landmark in the history of the nineteenth-century corn law, and to the student of Huskisson's work has a special importance, for he drew up its report. It may be considered the result of his careful investigation of the corn law problem. In addition to Huskisson, the leading members of the committee were Gooch, Castle-

[1] Hansard, 2nd ser., I. 535.

[2] *Annual Register*, 1821, 66.

reagh, Ricardo, Robinson, Brougham, and Parnell. It sat for fourteen weeks, took considerable evidence, and produced a report that left untouched few aspects of the subject. The *Annual Register* referred to it enthusiastically as 'one of the most valuable documents ever laid before Parliament. It is full of the soundest views; and at the same time as it admits abstract principles in all their extent, it modifies them by due regard to circumstances of the times.' [1]

The report frankly admitted that the complaints of the agriculturists were founded on fact 'in so far as they represent that, at the present price of corn, the returns to the occupier of an arable farm, after allowing for the interest of his investment, are by no means adequate to the charges and out-goings'.[2] Owing to a number of concurrent causes, farming had ceased to be remunerative. The returns of farming capital were considerably below the ordinary rate of profit. In examining the causes of this situation the committee drew attention first to the effect of the resumption of cash payments upon markets; the derangement thus caused was enhanced by the fact that other countries, simultaneously with Britain, reverted to a metallic currency. Yet the currency was not, as Western and other agriculturists erroneously stated, the chief cause of low corn prices. Of more vital effect was the redundant supply of grain in the British market. Tooke, one of the witnesses, pointed out that any corn over that which supplied every individual in a community was an absolute drug on the market; a succession of two or three abundant seasons must produce an inconvenient accumulation. Such was then the situation in England, for there had been a succession of good seasons.[3] The committee were confident that with an average crop the annual produce of corn was roughly equal to the annual consumption. When in good seasons the average was exceeded, the surplus con-

[1] *Annual Register*, 1821, 68.

[2] For the report see Hansard, 2nd ser., 5, app. lxix.

[3] For an admirable treatment of the effect of the seasons upon prices, see Tooke, *History of Prices* (1838), vol. i.

stituted the chief cause of low prices. No relief was possible by export to the continent, because there the supply was generally abundant and prices were low. The only remedy was the normal adjustment of the supply to the demand, either by the diminution of the one or the increase of the other. A further cause of agricultural depression was the sudden transition from the economic conditions of war to those of peace. The war had been a temporary stimulus to farming, and the withdrawal of this stimulus in the years following 1815 brought an inevitable depression commensurate in its magnitude to the former excitement. The committee believed that time alone would bring the necessary readjustment and relief.

But the committee were not content with general explanations. They brought the existing corn law under keen scrutiny, and placed upon it much of the blame for the depressed condition of agriculture. As Harriet Martineau wrote, Huskisson pulled down the image of clay which he himself had assisted to set up. A steady price was essential for the welfare of the landlord, tenant, and consumer. Under the law of 1815 such a price remained a dream. Rapid fluctuations were accentuated by the maintenance of an absolute prohibition of import up to a certain price, and an unlimited competition beyond. Thus, the evils of scarcity were aggravated, and the depression of price due to abundance was rendered more severe. Moreover, the existing law tended to deceive the grower with the false hope of monopoly, and held out to the country the prospect of an occasional free trade,

> 'but so regulated and desultory, as to baffle the calculations and unsettle the transactions, both of the grower and the dealer at home. . . . It exposes the markets of the country, either to be occasionally overwhelmed with an inundation of foreign corn, altogether disproportionate to its wants; or in the event of any considerable deficiency in our own harvest, it creates a sudden competition on the continent, by the effect of which, the prices there are rapidly and unnecessarily raised against ourselves.' [1]

An instance was given of the rapid fluctuations in price: in

[1] Hansard, 2nd ser., 5, app. lxxxii.

the seventeen months which passed between January 1816 and June 1817, the price of wheat jumped from *53s. 1d.* to *112s. 7d.* Such a violent ascent was due to a bad season, accentuated by the corn law which impeded necessary readjustments of supply to demand.

The above damaging criticisms were reinforced by another. The existing system had 'a direct tendency to contract the extent of our commercial dealings with other states, and to excite in the rulers of these a spirit of permanent exclusion against the productions or manufactures of this country'.[1] Trade as an exchange of equivalents could not expand if Britain persisted in prohibiting the free importation of continental grain. Huskisson here touched upon the argument developed by the economist M'Culloch and used on all occasions by the manufacturers, that free trade in corn was a *sine qua non* of British industrial development. Poland could not purchase Lancashire cottons unless Britain bought Polish corn. The logic of Cobden and the eloquence of Bright used this argument to attain in 1846 the repeal of the corn laws.

The committee subjected the complaints of the agriculturists to a critical examination. They pointed out that a fog of misconception prevailed as to the nature of a remunerative price. Many petitioners assumed that *80s.* a quarter was necessary to remunerate the farmer, and they desired a protective system to maintain the price at this level. The committee took pains to point out that it was impossible through protection to maintain grain at such a price: 'Protection cannot be carried further than monopoly. This monopoly the British owner has enjoyed for the produce of the two last harvests.' It was not the grain from abroad that depressed the market but the redundancy of supply at home. To the claim that the agriculturists were over-burdened with taxes the committee retorted that the price of corn was not determined by the amount of taxation, and it was the low price of corn which was the source of agricultural depression. 'The cost of growing corn in any country is regulated by the

[1] Hansard, 2nd ser., 5, app. lxxxii.

amount of capital necessary to produce it upon lands paying no rent, and that it is the price of the portion of corn which is so raised that determines the price of all other corn.' [1] Furthermore, agriculture had no more reason to be freed from taxation than had other industries, on which similar burdens fell. The claim of many petitioners that it should obtain the same protection as the leading manufactures was rejected. Most duties on imported goods were meant to countervail internal duties on the home manufactures. Such was the duty on glass. Moreover, the committee were inclined to believe that few manufactures, with the exception of silk, derived benefit from protection. It was obvious that industries which were competing successfully with foreign rivals need not fear opposition in their home market. Finally, the committee believed that the charges of the agriculturists against the warehousing in the United Kingdom of foreign grain lacked weight. There was a strong case for the warehousing of foreign grain, since it was removed from the reach of European states and ready on occasion to serve British needs.

The committee suggested remedies. They considered that the ideal corn law should consist of a fixed duty 'such as might compensate to the grower the loss of that encouragement which he received during the late war from the obstacles thrown in the way of free importation, and thereby protect the capitals now vested in agriculture from an unequal competition in the home market'. The fixed duty should countervail the difference of expense at which corn in the United Kingdom could be grown and marketed compared with the expense of producing and bringing it from European countries. But the committee timidly drew back from recommending the immediate enactment of such a duty, fearing that the supply in continental ports would add to the glut on the market. The immediate problem was to rectify the abuses of the existing law. To this end the committee suggested a lower price at which foreign corn could enter, and the imposition of a fixed duty

[1] *Ibid.* xcv.

upon the entrance of corn above that price. Such an alteration would check extravagant speculation and extensive importation, and benefit consumer and grower. Careful attention was shown to the interests of occupiers on the poorest and most expensive soils, and it was recommended that the legislature should preserve 'to the landed interest, the weight, station, and ascendancy, which it has enjoyed so long and used so beneficially'.

The report throws a vivid light upon the working of the corn law of 1815. No other public document between 1815 and 1846 is more illuminating. The laws of 1822 and 1828 were largely based on its general recommendations. Furthermore, it represented Huskisson's profession of faith. It showed clearly that he had shifted his moorings within the preceding year. As late as May 1820 he stated that the law of 1815 'had, in his opinion, answered the purposes for which it was intended'. But Huskisson, like Peel and Gladstone, was a ceaseless learner, ever open to the logic of facts. A careful investigation convinced him that the existing system worked badly and that its reform was imperative. The criticisms in the report of the law of 1815 distinctly represented his views. He had swung round to the position of Ricardo, by whom he was influenced on the committee, and now believed that instead of the existing system 'the safest mode would be to allow a free trade in corn, subject to a fair protecting duty'. This recommendation was his anchor in the succeeding years. Although he had no wish to maintain the British market as a monopoly to the British landowners, at the same time he did not accept the undiluted free-trade ideas tirelessly advanced by M'Culloch in the *Edinburgh Review*. What he meant by free trade was freedom to import, not freedom from duty. He wished to sponge from the corn law the prohibitive element which it had embodied since 1815. Beyond that, he had little wish to go. He saw a strong case for a moderate protective duty on the ground that England ought not to depend upon foreigners for its food supply. This idea remained an important ingredient in his national economy.

Huskisson's report did not satisfy the agriculturists. Their leaders on the committee, strongly dissenting, withdrew from the final sessions. Their irritation was expressed with unwonted eloquence by a Dr. Tucker of Devon who stated that the only remedy prescribed for the agricultural distress was patience:

'Admirable physicians! Admirable remedy! As if patience would discharge the rent of the landlord, satisfy the cravings of the tax-gatherer, and maintain the poor. But to talk of patience to the agriculturists when labouring under the weight of extreme distress —when they saw ruin breaking the hour-glass of time, and seizing its scythe to destroy their peace and property, was to add insult to injury.'[1]

The remarks of other critics might be less eloquent but were no less denunciatory.

In other quarters praise and criticism were more equally distributed. In the great Whig organ, the *Edinburgh Review*, M'Culloch commented that the report

'evinces a familiar acquaintance with many of the soundest, though not the most obvious, principles of economical science, and is on the whole, liberal and enlightened. The principles laid down by the committee all conspire to establish the injustice and impolicy of restricting the trade in corn. But instead of recommending, as they ought in consistency to have done, that the restrictions should be abolished, and the trade thrown open, the committee suggest that such a fixed duty should be imposed on the importation of foreign corn as might compensate the grower for the loss of that encouragement which he received during the late war. . . . In making this supposition, Mr. Huskisson, who framed the report, has doubtless sacrificed his own better judgement to the prejudices of the majority of the committee.'[2]

Joseph Lowe ranked the report 'among the most important and instructive documents of the kind that have appeared for many years', and declared that he subscribed to its doctrines 'with all who acknowledge the principles of free trade, and who lament that our legislature has deviated from them so materially in the case of our corn-

[1] *The Times*, 4 February 1822.

[2] *Edinburgh Review*, February 1822.

laws'.[1] Its most acute critic was Ricardo, who sat on the committee, but had not accepted in their entirety the statements and conclusions of Huskisson.[2] Although he placed the report in value alongside those on bullion and the resumption of cash payments, his free-trade instincts were outraged by the description of countervailing duties. He considered that it was profoundly misleading to consider them as duties equal to the additional expense of growing corn in this country over other countries. On this principle they might run as high as 30 per cent. His conception of countervailing duties was that of imposts to subject the foreigner to the taxational burdens borne by the home grower. In the same speech Ricardo stated his own guiding principle—the slogan cry of free traders in the succeeding thirty years—that 'the only true policy was to allow us to go to the country where the article required was most easily and abundantly produced'.[3]

Immediate action on the report was not taken. The agrarian distress lingered, and a steady stream of petitions from agricultural districts continued. 'Abundance of every kind of agricultural produce', remarked *The Times*, 'is said to occasion the present distress. Of one thing we are certain, there is abundance of agricultural resolutions.'[4] Creevey remarked that 'landlords and farmers seem to have no other occupation than comparing their respective distresses'.[5] In Parliament Huskisson was the special object of attack by irritated landlords. Hence on the reappointment of the committee in the following year, Huskisson, in order to allow them to come to independent conclusions did not attend. The second report adopted substantially the conclusions of the first. A struggle now ensued within Parliament between those favourable to free trade in corn and those who saw national salvation only in high protective duties. The division in Parliament had its counterpart within the Government. Lord Castlereagh moved resolutions based on the report of the second

[1] Lowe, *State of the Nation*, app. ch. v (1822).

[2] Hansard, 2nd ser., 6. 1446.

[3] Hansard, 2nd ser., 6. 1448.

[4] *The Times*, 6 May 1822.

[5] *Creevey Papers*, ii. 51.

agricultural committee.[1] Huskisson disagreed with them, and moved counter resolutions. Castlereagh's chief suggestions, upon which the corn law of 1822 rested, were briefly that the ports be opened when the home price reached 80*s.* and continued open until it descended below 70*s.*; when the price was between 70*s.* and 80*s.*, the duty was to be 12*s.*, and an additional duty of 5*s.* during the first three months of importation; a duty of 5*s.* when the price of corn was between 80*s.* and 85*s.*; above 85*s.* a duty of only 1*s.* Colonial preference was recognized as in the former law. It is significant that under the new law foreign importation was totally prohibited until home corn reached 70*s.*; beyond that price a sliding scale restrained foreign competition. This construction of checks and balances might seem a concession to a freer trade, but in reality its ultimate effect was similar to the Act of 1815. M'Culloch in the *Edinburgh Review* considered it 'a second though certainly not improved edition of that of 1815'.

Huskisson's counter proposals differed in one important respect from Castlereagh's. They rested on the idea that British ports should always be open to foreign corn. Huskisson sought by allowing free import to facilitate an easy and regular corn trade between Britain and the continent. He had the same end in view when in 1814 he moved an amendment to Parnell's resolutions. He considered that prohibition of import up to a specified price would invariably 'expose sometimes the grower of corn to the losses incident to an over-redundant produce, and at other times the consumer to the pressure inseparable from dearth'.[2] Not merely were the home producers and consumers injured but the merchants found importation precarious, and hence British trade suffered. Huskisson's remedial proposals, rejected by the protectionists, rested on the principles of the law of 1773. In his eleventh resolution he stated that 'trade in foreign corn shall thenceforth be permanently free; but subject to the following duties upon importation, or when taken out of warehouse

[1] Hansard, 2nd ser., 7. 190.

[2] *Speeches*, ii. 121.

for home consumption:—wheat, 15*s.* a quarter, when the price shall not exceed 80*s.*; and when above that price, 5*s.*; and above 85*s.* one shilling'.[1] The other grains had duties proportional. As a preliminary to the establishment of such a system, Huskisson suggested that the corn in bond might be allowed to enter first at the 15*s.* duty when the home price reached 70*s.*; three months later wheat from abroad might be admitted. But the agriculturists and the ultra-Tories in the Government were powerful, and Huskisson's suggestions were not accepted.

After 1822 the agricultural depression slowly tended to pass, but not the fears and activities of the agrarian party. It became patent that the corn law existed on duress. Huskisson's suggestion that free trade, with only such restrictions as would protect the home grower for the difficulties under which he cultivated, gripped the minds of many parliamentarians. A change in the existing system was inevitable. Within the Government Canning and Huskisson frankly stated that the law of 1822 was not final. But Huskisson, in keeping with his general political philosophy of reform by slow steps, did not attempt to alter radically the existing law. In February 1823 he remarked that 'any important alteration in the corn laws could not be made with a partial and limited discussion, and a temporary investigation; for, in the present state of the agriculturists, which he was sorry to say was the reverse of what he should wish it to be, no alteration could now be made, which would accommodate the various opinions of those who were interested. Few were agreed as to the particular remedy'.[2]

In his estimation it would be valueless, even if possible, to carry a law which had not strong support amongst the class most affected. Yet he was prepared to modify the existing system, and in 1824 carried a change respecting the warehousing of wheat. At this time, Hamburgh and Dantzic supplied the British West Indies with flour. Huskisson saw the advantage of allowing the corn bonded in warehouses to be taken out, converted into flour, and then

[1] *Speeches*, ii. 122.

[2] *Ibid.* 172.

returned to warehouses for shipment to the West Indies. But the agriculturists, fearing that such flour might filter into the home market, were inclined to oppose this suggestion. Huskisson quieted their fears by pointing out that they as landowners would benefit.

'The tubs, hoops, &c., in which flour came from Dantzic, were formed in that country, and gave employment to a vast number or industrious mechanics. If we allowed foreign corn to be ground in this country, and afterwards exported from it, the tubs which contained it must be formed of staves taken from the demesnes of English gentlemen, and wrought into shape by the industry of their tenantry. He did not see any reason why, with our extensive colonial connexion, we should not appropriate to ourselves that trade which was at present carried on very lucratively by foreigners.' [1]

The argument was convincing, and his measure was carried.

In 1825 Huskisson became emphatic in his criticism of the existing system. On April 28 he delivered a powerful speech condemning with scant restraint the established corn law, and the opinions of Gooch its supporter.

'The great desideratum in this important question was to provide for a steadiness of price, and to guard against excessive fluctuations in it from the vicissitudes of trade. How did the present law provide for these ends? By limiting the markets from which we drew our supplies—by destroying the vent which we should otherwise have for our produce, whenever we were blessed with a superabundant harvest—and by exposing us to an alternate fluctuation of high and low prices. To say of a system which affected the price of labour and the comforts of the labourer, and which cramped the resources, not only of the manufacturer, but also of the farmer himself . . . that it 'worked well', was an assertion so completely refuted by the report of 1821, that he was surprised that any man should be bold enough to make it.' [2]

After such condemnation it would seem only consistent that Huskisson should attain what he had recommended in 1821 and what 'he had hoped to see yet accomplished, a free trade in corn, under a proper and due protection'. But two considerations kept him from recommending fresh legislation. The first and stronger was a

[1] *Ibid.* 280.

[2] *Ibid.* 395.

large supply of cheap corn in the ports of Europe. If the laws allowed freer import, the continental supply would move like an avalanche into the British market, and temporarily crush out the British farmer. But within a year's time the glut might sufficiently disappear to allow new legislation. The other consideration that deterred him, although it found no expression in his parliamentary utterances, was that the ultra-Tory and agricultural wing of the Liverpool Government would not tolerate a thorough reform. In 1825–6 the ministry was frequently on the brink of collapse. A corn law allowing free trade would have precipitated a ministerial division which even Lord Liverpool's supreme tact could not have healed. Hence it was prudent to wait.

Throughout the nation opinion favourable to Huskisson's views was steadily strengthening. *The Times* espoused the cause of free trade, and expressed pleasure with the fact that the manufacturing towns and districts sought a revision of the corn laws.

> 'There is no end', ran one of its editorials, 'to the variety of mischiefs brought upon the nation by this cruel tax on bread. It adds a third to the wages of labour in all branches, and lessens, in the same ratio those manufactured exports, which form the subject matter of our competition with foreign states in peace, and furnish the best source of protection against them when they become our enemies. The corn law adds a full third to the expenses of the landowner himself, not merely in the support of his house, but in the management and cultivation of his property.' [1]

A short but intense wave of commercial depression overtook the country in 1825–6, and gave added force to the arguments of the manufacturers. The publication of Jacob's report in 1826 had greater effect.[2] Jacob travelled and investigated conditions in the corn-growing countries of the Baltic. He reported to the Privy Council that in the event of Britain removing her restrictive corn laws, no great increase in the quantity of wheat from the Baltic might be expected. The British landowners need fear

[1] *The Times*, 21 November 1825.

[2] For Jacob's report see Hansard, 15. 400.

little competition from continental cultivators, because under existing conditions the latter were producing their maximum supply of cheap grain. The effects of the report were electric. Such convinced protectionists as Parnell became free traders, and it provided M'Culloch of the *Edinburgh Review* with fresh ammunition to discharge at the hitherto invulnerable corn law.[1]

Meanwhile, Huskisson and Canning silently bored breaches in the established system. With masterly tactics they undermined the foundations of a law which they dared not directly attack. In June 1825 Huskisson carried two important Bills: one allowed foreign corn in warehouses to be admitted for a limited time at the duty of 10*s*., moderate enough to encourage importers to bring corn into the market;[2] the other allowed the free importation of Canadian corn for a period of two years.[3] To calm the fears of British agriculturists he remarked that not more than an average of 50,000 or 60,000 quarters of corn had been annually imported from Canada, a very negligible amount. At the very most Canada could not send any more than 100,000 quarters.[4] He also took occasion to appeal to the shipping interests and the imperial instincts of the House of Commons:

> 'To bring this to England would cause the employment of from twenty to thirty thousand tons of British shipping; and when the importance of our relations between that colony and our own country were duly considered, and the jealous commercial rivalry of the United States of America also taken into the scale, he was sure the importance of fostering the interests of Canada would appear in a strong light.'[5]

The measure reflected the ever-present desire of Huskisson to advance colonial interests and through them the interests of the Empire as a whole.

The industrial depression of 1826 with the consequent pressure upon the working classes provided Huskisson with an additional reason for making changes in the corn

1 For Parnell's recantation see Hansard, 16. 1101.

2 6 Geo. IV, c. 65.

3 6 Geo. IV, c. 64.

4 *Speeches*, ii. 406.

5 *Ibid.* 407.

law. In May he and Canning introduced resolutions with the purpose of alleviating the distress of the industrial classes. One resolution was that 250,000 quarters of corn in bond should be allowed to enter the market free of duty. The other, no less important, was to empower the Government during the summer recess to allow a partial or general free importation of corn, as necessity might require. Both measures, Huskisson argued, were dictated by an emergency. He pleaded innocence of any design to render the corn law nugatory. The Government's proposals were framed only to relieve an urgent distress that affected particularly the powerful cotton industry: 'If a foreign demand could be created, either by the purchase of corn, or by any similar measure, relief would be administered to the cotton manufacturer'. This was the sharp blade of the free-trade argument, and although Huskisson only used it in a crisis, it was never far from his reach. The smooth marketing of Lancashire cottons rested upon the purchase by Britain of continental corn. With Cobden this argument was a reason for the removal of all duties on corn. Huskisson saw its worth, but he was in a different situation and was a different man from Cobden. He had not Cobden's unwavering conviction that England must be turned into an industrial workshop. Only when British industry seemed impaired as in 1826 did he put the argument into use.

Notwithstanding the reassuring remarks of Huskisson and Canning, the landowners forced a vigorous debate on the resolutions. But on this occasion the agricultural interest went down to defeat. The passage of the two Bills was of profound significance.[1] Creevey's characteristic comments are sufficiently illuminating: 'It certainly is the boldest thing that ever was attempted by a government—after deprecating any discussion on the corn laws during the present session, to try at the end of it to carry a corn law of their own by a *coup de main*, and to hold out the landed grandees as the enemies of the manufacturing population if they oppose it—the charm of the power of the landed interest is gone; and in a new Parliament

[1] 7 Geo. IV, cc. 70 and 71.

Canning and Huskisson may effect whatever revolution they like in the corn laws.'[1]

In 1827 Creevey's prophecy seemed on the eve of fulfilment. Canning and Huskisson endeavoured to carry a new Corn Bill. It embodied the sliding scale, and was designed to provide an adequate protection to the home grower, because as Huskisson argued 'nothing can be so dangerous to this country' as reliance on foreign countries for their supplies of corn. In keeping with Huskisson's liberalism, it was a moderate advance towards that freer trade which he had long advocated and had recommended in the report of 1821. Sixty shillings was taken as the pivot price, up to which the home growers were allowed what he considered adequate protection. At 60*s*. a duty of 20*s*. was to be imposed; as the home price dropped below 60*s*. the duty would increase—a 2*s*. increase in the duty for every 1*s*. drop in price; for every 1*s*. increase above the price 60*s*. the duty was to drop 2*s*., and thus gradually the duty would fall to zero. A very significant fact respecting this proposal is that at no price foreign corn would be prohibited. Thus the element of prohibition, embodied in the laws of 1815 and 1822, was thrown overboard. Huskisson built upon his suggestions in the report of 1821, and endeavoured to revive the system of 1773, to provide a steady and smooth corn trade between Britain and the continent. Under his arrangement there would normally be no interruption to the transport of Lancashire cottons to Poland and Prussia, in exchange for Polish and Prussian corn. But the fears of the agriculturists were aroused. The graduated scale might, they suspected, fail to provide sufficient protection. In the Lords, the Duke of Wellington was the stubborn champion of the landlords, and moved an amendment with respect to the warehousing of corn that wrecked the Bill.[2] Huskisson had to be content with a temporary measure for the admission of bonded corn.[3] The agriculturists in Parliament were obviously stronger than Creevey had prophesied.

[1] *Creevey Papers*, ii. 100.

[2] Hansard, N.S. 17. 1231.

[3] 7 and 8 Geo. IV, c. 57.

But a new corn law was inevitable. However strong the agriculturists might be, they could not preserve the existing system against the insistent pressure of the new industrial classes. No sooner was Wellington's ministry formed in 1828 than it grappled with the task of framing a law satisfactory to the diverse elements in the Government and respectable in the eyes of a critical community. Huskisson was not directly responsible for the Bill. He had gone to the Colonial Office, and Grant, who became President of the Board of Trade, introduced the measure. But Huskisson, we learn from Ellenborough's *Diary*, was very active in shaping it in the Cabinet meetings. He contended vigorously for a system similar to that proposed in 1827. It was inevitable that the new law would be, as Grant described it, 'an arbitration or compromise between conflicting interests and opinions'. Yet it embodied the main principles of Huskisson's proposal of the former year. Foreign grain was free to enter British ports at all times subject to a duty framed on a sliding scale not very different from that in the former year. A limited recognition was given to a fixed duty long advocated by Huskisson. After home prices of wheat had reached 73*s*. the sliding scale ceased, and a fixed duty of 1*s*. was imposed. The proposed measure of 1827 and the Bill of 1828 may best be compared in the following schedules:

When home price was	*1827 duty was*	*1828 duty was*
52*s*.	40*s*. 8*d*.	34*s*. 8*d*.
53*s*.	38*s*. 8*d*.	33*s*. 8*d*.
54*s*.	36*s*. 8*d*.	32*s*. 8*d*.
55*s*.	34*s*. 8*d*.	31*s*. 8*d*.
56*s*.	32*s*. 8*d*.	30*s*. 8*d*.
57*s*.	30*s*. 8*d*.	29*s*. 8*d*.
58*s*.	28*s*. 8*d*.	28*s*. 8*d*.
59*s*.	26*s*. 8*d*.	27*s*. 8*d*.
60*s*.	24*s*. 8*d*.	26*s*. 8*d*.
61*s*.	22*s*. 8*d*.	25*s*. 8*d*.
62*s*.	20*s*. 8*d*.	24*s*. 8*d*.
63*s*.	18*s*. 8*d*.	23*s*. 8*d*.
64*s*.	16*s*. 8*d*.	22*s*. 8*d*.
65*s*.	14*s*. 8*d*.	21*s*. 8*d*.
66*s*.	12*s*. 8*d*.	20*s*. 8*d*.

When home price was	*1827 duty was*	*1828 duty was*
67*s.*	10*s.* 8*d.*	18*s.* 8*d.*
68*s.*	6*s.* 8*d.*	16*s.* 8*d.*
69*s.*	4*s.* 8*d.*	12*s.* 8*d.*
70*s.*	2*s.* 8*d.*	10*s.* 8*d.*
71*s.*	1*s.*	6*s.* 8*d.*
72*s.*	1*s.*	2*s.* 8*d.*
73*s.*	1*s.*	—

Huskisson preferred the new scale because it provided more protection to the agriculturists. He pointed out that a duty of 20*s.* when home price was 60*s.* as proposed in 1827 was not adequate protection. One is inclined to question the candidness of such argument. Huskisson had fought for the most effective measure possible, and on his own confession did not think the new one 'the best which might have been brought forward', but a wise opportunism led him to defend the proposed system, since a better was not at the time attainable. It is worth noting that Baring considered that the new law would be less favourable to agriculture because more protection was required when the home price was from 52*s.* to 58*s.* than when it was from 62*s.* to 68*s.* With the new scale, when the price was low, the protection would be diminished; when high, increased. In this manner Huskisson won a subtle conquest over Wellington and the agricultural party.

Although a compromise, the new law remained on the statute book until modified by Peel in 1843. It was the last measure with which Huskisson as minister was concerned. Indeed he had resigned from Wellington's ministry before the Bill passed the Commons.

Huskisson's attitude towards the corn laws was one of development. Out of consideration for the needs of Britain in the transition from war to peace he was first a high protectionist. The interests vested in agriculture must not light-heartedly be sacrificed. Moreover, Britain could not gamble with her food supply. Security of food resources was the life-blood of the nation, and such security depended upon the maintenance of home production. Such were the chief considerations which made him the champion of the Act of 1815. But Huskisson, open to the teaching of facts, had by 1821 reached the conclusion that the existing law did not fulfil the ends for which it had been established. Monopoly up to a specified price and free trade beyond were conducive to violent price fluctuations, and provided the agriculturists with an illusionary protection. Hence Huskisson sought to secure free import with a protective duty. In other words, he aimed to sweep away prohibition which injured British farmers and consumers, as well as rendered impossible a steady exchange of industrial products for continental grain. His vision for Great Britain was national self-sufficiency combined with industrial and commercial expansion. The ideal of an economically self-contained nation demanded protection for agriculture, the essential industry of national existence. But high protection for agriculture hampered the development of a Britain powerful in industries, in ships, and in commerce. The basis of trade is the free exchange of equivalents, and such exchange would be injured by barriers to the import of foreign agricultural products. Huskisson's compromise reflects his endeavour to reconcile these two ideals. He saw in the sliding scale an expedient that might satisfy in part two imperative needs.

His system, however, was a very defective contrivance for the protection of British agriculture. Juggling with the duties of a sliding scale was of little genuine benefit. Some years later M'Culloch forcibly pointed out that the sliding scale was in its effects positively evil:[1] (i) It doubled the hazards of trade in corn, and accentuated fluctuations in price. When prices were rising it tempted foreign merchants to hold back their grain in the expectation of entering it at a reduced duty. On the other hand, when a fall of prices was anticipated, the market became overloaded and prices ruinously depressed. Thus the system brought privations to the manufacturers by encouraging importers to withhold corn till the price attained a high level. For the agriculturists it brought injury by making importers throw their grain on a market already depressed. (ii) The system similarly injured British trade

[1] M'Culloch, *Commercial Dictionary* (ed. 1880), 442–4.

transactions. There was a demand one year for about ten times the quantity of Polish corn required the next year, but the Poles could not reciprocate by taking ten times the quantity of cottons and woollens, and hence the excess was frequently paid for in bullion, with results often injurious to financial interests. Much better would it have been for British agriculture and commerce had Huskisson staked everything upon realizing his proposal of 1821, free trade with a moderate, fixed duty. His desire to save vested interests and his attempts to combine two contradictory principles led him into a corn law policy that advanced neither the interests of agriculture nor of manufacturing. He would have been saved from such a policy had he sufficiently heeded in 1821 Ricardo's criticism of the sliding scale.[1]

The difference in Huskisson's position from that of the free traders of later years was apparent. With Cobden, the man most responsible for the removal of the corn laws, he was in sharp contrast. Cobden's logical mind was largely content with visualizing one objective for Britain, the attainment of industrial power through the expansion of British markets. There was much truth in the description of him as 'the inspired bagman who believes in a cotton millennium'.[2] His sagacious intellect was conscious of the complexity of national needs, but he was too much of an apostle to avoid the belief that these complex needs could be satisfied by one policy. He was prepared to sacrifice agriculture to manufacturing, and this sacrifice he pushed upon Britain. Huskisson shared with Malthus an unwillingness to see England become merely an industrialized community dependent on foreigners for its bread. He had been trained in statesmanship within those years when the storm of war devastated Europe, and he had then been taught the value of national self-containment, a lesson that he did not shed, and one which restrained him from advocating an unlimited free trade in grain.

1 For Ricardo's remarks on the sliding scale see Hansard, 2nd ser., 4. 1157.

2 Gibbon, C., *Life of George Combe*, ii. 309 (2 vols. Portsmouth, 1878).

Yet Huskisson's final opinion on corn duties was not very unlike that maintained by the champions of the Anti-Corn-Law League. In March 1830 he declared that it was 'his unalterable conviction that we could not uphold the corn laws now in existence, together with the present taxation, and at the same time increase national prosperity, and preserve public contentment. That those laws might be repealed without affecting the landed interest, whilst at the same time the distress of the people might be relieved, he never had any doubt whatever.'[1] Thus even in the last two years of his life he was prepared to change his opinions, if facts seemed to warrant it. It was his conclusion that the existing law, with the sliding scale which he had helped to establish, failed to serve any purpose. It seriously hampered British trade with the United States and other countries, and its vaunted protection to agriculture was now unnecessary, since the Jacob reports had demonstrated that there need be no fear of an avalanche of continental corn entering the British market under a system of the open door. The Baltic countries were already producing their maximum of cheap corn, and the demand for an increased output would so raise the cost of production as to enable the British farmer to compete readily with his continental rivals. Huskisson had thus traversed the whole gamut of opinion on the corn law issue. His policy had moved with Britain's growing needs for wider markets and a readily obtainable food supply. He was throughout influenced more by the logic of fact than by the logic of theory. How his attitude towards the corn laws had its counterpart in his attitude towards other aspects of the protectionist system must be examined in succeeding chapters.

[1] *Speeches*, iii. 55.

IV

THE FIRST BREACHES IN THE OLD COMMERCIAL SYSTEM

THE commercial system with which Great Britain entered the nineteenth century was an intricate mosaic structure. It consisted of innumerable Acts and regulations, many of which dated at least from the sixteenth century and conformed to no principle except that of protecting and shaping the economic resources of the nation for the attainment of political power. A committee in 1820 discovered that there were some 2,000 Acts affecting trade, and of these 1,500 were in force in 1815. Not merely commerce but agriculture and industry felt the influence of parliamentary enactments. We have already seen how agriculture received the protection of the corn laws. Efforts no less vigorous were made to promote the growth of manufactures by high duties and prohibitions, and the exportation of machinery was prohibited in order that the product of English invention might not enrich continental rivals. Skilled workmen were prevented by heavy penalties from emigrating to other lands, in order that foreigners might not acquire those industrial arts which brought economic power to Great Britain. There were also statutes minutely regulating the details of production in many industries, some of which belonged to the reign of Elizabeth. But the most representative measures of the mercantile state were the navigation regulations. While the industrial changes of the eighteenth century reduced the measures affecting manufactures to little more than dead timber, the Navigation Acts remained the flourishing oaks of British policy, unbowed and little disturbed by the changes of a century and a half. At the beginning of 1822 they were substantially intact. With few changes they were the same laws that the ministers of Charles II had established and that the advisers of William III had finally fashioned. They held a unique place in British policy.

Throughout the eighteenth century they were generally acclaimed the essential foundation of British commercial and marine power. They were considered the nursing mother of the nation's naval strength. Even Adam Smith, who found much to criticize in mercantilism and who saw dire economic consequences resulting from the navigation laws, held the opinion that they represented great political wisdom. Defence was of more importance than opulence. Yet these vital laws were virtually the first object of attack by the reformers of the twenties, and the most important of Huskisson's labours was his dominant share in their modification.

The famous Act of 1660 constituted the foundation of the navigation code.[1] It might be considered the 'fortieth' article of the religion of the state. Upon it was built a large series of supplementary Acts and amendments, but its own clauses remained the basic provisions with respect to imperial shipping. At the risk of relating facts discussed in general histories a summary of the chief clauses of the Navigation Act must be sketched as a necessary background to the reforms with which Huskisson's name is associated. The sub-title explains that the Act is 'for the encouragement and increasing of shipping and navigation'. Like its predecessors, in the reign of Richard II, it rested on the assumption that ships were like gold coins, they would disappear if measures were not taken to encourage and maintain them. There could be no assurance of a navy without protection to mercantile shipping, and upon it depended the very existence of Britain. The famous Act of Charles II's reign therefore provided that (i) No goods were to be imported from the plantations but in English ships. With such a provision a colonial empire became the veritable means of creating a navy, as reversely a powerful navy was essential for the maintenance of an empire. (ii) No goods of the growth, production, or manufacture of Africa, Asia, or America were to be imported into England, Ireland, or Wales except in vessels that belong to the people of England, Ireland, Wales, or a

[1] 12 Car. II, c. 18.

British colony. The master and three-fourths of the crew must also be English mariners. (iii) English ships were not to bring foreign goods of Asia, Africa, or America except directly from the place of their growth or manufacture. This provision was of course to encourage the 'long haul' of goods from distant places in English ships and discourage the carrying trade of England's rivals, the Dutch. (iv) No goods were to be carried from one port of England to another in the vessel of an alien. (v) Goods of the growth or manufacture of Muscovy were to be imported only in English ships. A similar provision concerned goods from the Turkish Empire, 'except only such foreign ships and vessels as are of the build of that country or place of which the said goods are the growth, production, or manufacture respectively, or of such port where the said goods can only be, or most usually are first shipped for transportation'. (vi) Certain products of the British colonies were not to be shipped to any foreign country, but must be sent directly to England, whence some of the commodities might later be sent abroad. The goods mentioned were sugars, tobaccos, cotton-wool, indigo, ginger, and fustick. Such was the famous enumeration list which allowed British merchants to have a pre-emption over foreigners of the major products of the colonies.

In the succeeding ten years Acts were passed supplementary to that of 1660. One of the most important was the statute for preventing frauds and regulating abuses in His Majesty's customs.[1] With the obvious aim of injuring the commerce of Holland it prohibited the importation on any vessels of a long list of staple wares into England from the Netherlands or Germany, and declared that a foreign-built ship could not become British by purchase. Other Acts whose importance increased with the growth of the Empire dealt with the plantation trade. Their aim was to shut out completely the Dutch and other foreign carriers from the inter-imperial trade and to direct all important colonial products to English ports. A self-sufficing Empire in matters pertaining to shipping and trade was the

[1] 13 and 14 Car. II, c. 11.

ideal of Stuart statesmen. A notable statute was that of 1663 which provided that no European goods should be brought into the plantations but what shall be shipped in England in English ships and carried directly to the plantations.[1] In other words, European goods must first be landed in England before exportation to the colonies and must then be sent in English vessels, a measure beneficial to the public revenue as well as to English carriers. Another Act[2] imposed on governors the duty of making annual returns of all ships lading commodities in the colonies, and a statute of 1672[3] had further details with respect to enumerated commodities. The Acts mentioned did not by any means constitute all of the famous navigation code. Amending measures were often passed, and in the reign of William III a very important statute dealt with inter-colonial trade.[4] But the main structure of the navigation system was erected in the reign of Charles II.

Until after the American Revolution no deep inroads were made in the system. Modifications were introduced,[5] particularly with respect to the plantations, but there was no substantial alteration in the general character of the code. Amongst the amendments of importance was the Free Port Act of 1766 which opened a slight breach in the restrictions on foreign vessels in British colonial ports.[6] It gave liberty to import in foreign vessels live cattle and goods, the produce of any foreign American colony into the island of Dominica and the ports of Jamaica, with the exception of some enumerated goods and foreign manufactures. It conceded that negroes imported into the two mentioned islands in British ships might be exported again in foreign vessels. Significantly the reason assigned in the preamble for this slight inroad into the navigation system is that the revenue of the Empire would benefit. The development of naval power was temporarily waived in favour of revenue. Much deeper

[1] 15 Car. II, c. 7.
[2] 22 and 23 Car. II, c. 26.
[3] 25 Car. II, c. 7.
[4] 7 and 8 William III, c. 22.
[5] See 13 Geo. I, c. 15; 7 Geo. II, c. 18; 14 Geo. II, c. 36; 20 Geo. III,
[6] 6 Geo. III, c. 49.

reasons underlay the changes with which Huskisson's name is associated, and they are partly explained by the most important event in the history of Britain's first Empire, the American Revolution. The conclusion of the revolutionary war in 1783 opened a new chapter in the story of the navigation system. The independence of the thirteen colonies shattered the territorial basis for the enactments of Charles II's reign, and created an impulse amongst British statesmen so to modify the Navigation Acts as to fit them into the new political situation. The thirteen colonies were independent foreign communities, and the extensive trade between them and the West Indies and Britain could no longer be maintained without changes in the provisions of the navigation code. What had been created under monopoly was now in danger of being destroyed under exclusion. If the old regulations were rigidly enforced, the British West Indies would lose their trade with the thirteen colonies, and the development of their economic life would seriously suffer, since the bulk of their commerce was with the mainland.

Both Fox and Pitt quickly grasped the situation. In the year of the peace Pitt endeavoured to carry a Bill that would allow American vessels admission to the ports of the West Indies with merchandise of American growth or produce, and would permit such vessels to export to the United States any goods whatever.[1] His measure received considerable support. The West Indian merchants were strong in its favour. Many publicists and public men pleaded for the admission of Americans to the commercial privileges of British subjects and claimed 'that the Navigation Act so long esteemed the palladium of the naval power of Britain, should be infringed by a free admission of their vessels into the ports of our West India islands. The press teemed with pamphlets written in support of these new maxims of commercial policy; and some of the governors of the islands in reality acted as if they thought the peace had placed the Americans precisely in the same condition they were in before the Revolution, and freely admitted

[1] See *Parliamentary History*, 23. 602, 639, 723.

them into their ports.'[1] Amongst the advocates of the new policy was Adam Smith, whose powerful mind thoroughly understood Britain's navigation code. He soundly argued that the United States should be admitted to the West Indies on the same terms as before the war, because 'the lumber and provisions of the United States are more necessary to our West India islands than the rum and sugar of the latter are to the former. Any interruption or restraint of commerce would hurt our loyal much more than our revolted subjects.'[2]

The opportune time had arrived for a sweeping change in the old commercial system, and it was Pitt's aim to effect it. But strong opposition, particularly from shipowners, quickly developed.[3] Eden, in the House of Commons, aroused the fears of many when he declared that Pitt's proposed Bill 'would introduce revolution in our commercial system, which he was afraid would shake it to its very basis and endanger the whole pile'.[4] Lord Sheffield published his influential pamphlet *Observations on the Commerce of the United States*, and it was followed by the work of Chalmers, *Opinions on Interesting Subjects of Public Law and Commercial Policy arising from American Independence*. These writers argued that there was no urgent reason why the regulations respecting the West Indian trade should be altered as Britain and Ireland, with the other British possessions in North America, were competent to supply the West India islands with lumber and provisions, if the revolted states should refuse to sell them such commodities. They believed that there was no serious menace in the threat of the United States to refuse admission to British merchandise 'because goods must ever find their market in proportion to their quality and practice, independent of all resolutions, and even laws'. In an age

[1] Macpherson, D., *Annals of Commerce*, iv. 18 (4 vols. London, 1805).

[2] Adam Smith to Mr. Eden. *Journal and Correspondence of Lord Auckland*, i. 64 (4 vols. London, 1861–2).

[3] See Burnet, E. C., 'London Merchants on American Trade', (*American Historical Review*, xviii. 769).

[4] *Parl. Hist.* 23. 602.

when smuggling was a normal means of exchange the last statement had more than an element of truth.

The opposition to Pitt's Bill was fatal, and an excellent opportunity of avoiding in the future much international friction was lost. Free trade between the British colonies and the American States was long postponed. But important modifications in the old arrangements were made. A statute allowed ministers to make necessary changes in the navigation regulations to facilitate 'the better carrying on of trade and commerce between the subjects of his Majesty's Dominions and the inhabitants of the United States'.[1] It bore fruit. A proclamation of 2 July 1783 permitted British subjects to carry in British vessels naval stores, spars, lumber, horses and other livestock, and all kinds of corn, flour, and bread, from the United States to the West Indian islands. They were also allowed to carry rum, sugar, molasses, coffee, chocolate, nuts, ginger, and pimento from the islands to the United States, on paying the duties and conforming to the same regulations as if they were cleared for a British colony. But the arrangement was satisfying neither to the West Indian planters nor to the United States. So long as American ships were prohibited a serious handicap was imposed on commerce, and throughout the succeeding decades the bone of contention between the American and British Governments was the carrying trade. The Government at Westminster, moved by the old spirit of mercantile imperialism, sought a monopoly for the British shipowners, although the West Indian planters were anxious to see American as well as British ships competing for their freights. To the planters competition was the sole guarantee of cheap freights and trade expansion. Their case was ably expounded in England by a West Indian, Brian Edwards, who addressed a pamphlet on the subject to Lord Sheffield.[2] He pointed out the impossibility for British ships to supply the sugar islands with American produce, except on terms ruinous

[1] 23 Geo. III, c. 39.

[2] *Thoughts on the Late Proceedings of Government Respecting the Trade of the West India Islands with the United States of America* (London, 1784).

either to the merchant who carried on the trade or to the planter. The reason was to be found in the cheapness of American shipping in comparison with that of Britain, a cheapness due to the facilities for shipbuilding in the United States. Moreover, by the exclusion of American vessels from the carrying trade, the West Indian planters lost the market of the republic, and for this loss the trade with the northern colonies could not compensate. The commerce of the Americans, argued Edwards, was more necessary to the West India islands than that of the islands to them, for Americans could get their sugar and rum in the French possessions, while the British planters could not find adequate markets elsewhere. This opinion was later established by statistics. In 1770 the West Indies had shipped to the mother country produce amounting to £3,279,204.[1] In 1787 the exports had risen to £4,839,145, a gain of over 30 per cent.[2] Between the same years exports to the United States had fallen from £481,407 to £196,461. The Americans had gone to the French islands for their rum and sugar. The problem that faced British statesmen was obvious. Were the motives which in the seventeenth century placed the navigation laws upon the statute book powerful enough in the era after the American Revolution to warrant the rigid maintenance of those laws, even at the risk of injury to imperial commerce? In other words, were colonial trade and prosperity to be sacrificed to ships? For the time being British ministers shrank from a decisive answer. In the twenties Huskisson and his colleagues laid the problem at rest by considering colonial trade and economic freedom as paramount to the interests of shipping.

Although in the interval the navigation laws remained sacred in the eyes of ministers, slight amendments were effected. One important concession was made by a proclamation of 1783 to the effect that goods from the United States might be imported into Great Britain in American as well as British vessels. An Act in 1797 gave parliamen-

[1] Macpherson, *Annals of Commerce*, iii. 506.

[2] *Ibid.* iv. 158.

tary sanction to this concession.[1] Of more significance was the provision in Jay's treaty, in 1794, that American vessels not above the burden of seventy tons might bring the produce of the United States to ports in the British West Indies.[2] The American senate refused to ratify this article, because unfortunately it was coupled with conditions which they repudiated, but Britain continued to allow the concession by executive order. As a matter of fact it was to her interest to do so. Owing to the war, British ships were required in European waters, and the entrance of small vessels to the West Indian trade proved a welcome assistance to British shipping. In 1805 the Imperial Government, following the precedent set by the statute of 1766, cut into the old system by establishing in certain colonies free ports, to which the vessels of foreign states might trade.[3] Among those created by the Act were St. Ann's in Jamaica; St. John's, Antigua; San Josef, Trinidad; Kingston, St. Vincent; Scarborough, Tobago; and the principal port in Bermuda. There were of course provisions respecting the commodities to be imported and exported. Some years later another Act extended the system of free ports to the Canadas, New Brunswick, Nova Scotia, Prince Edward Island, and Newfoundland, and also permitted direct trade between these colonies and European ports south of Finisterre.[4]

Such, briefly, were the chief inroads into the mercantile system previous to the twenties of the nineteenth century. In no way were they revolutionary. Substantially the Navigation Acts remained inviolate. The most important change was the establishment of the free ports. Shipping to and from the colonies remained the guarded preserve of British carriers, and the ideal of ships and colonies, each auxiliary to the other, still filled the vision of British statesmen. Colonies were considered primarily as the nursery of seamen. Proof of the high faith of the Imperial Govern-

[1] 37 Geo. III, c. 97.

[2] Art. XII, see text of treaty in *Treaties and Conventions Between the United States and Other Powers*, 318–32 (Washington, 1873).

[3] 45 Geo. III, c. 57.

[4] 49 Geo. III, c. 47.

ment in the navigation regulations is found in the rigid manner in which they forbade American ships to enter the West Indian trade. The concession granted in Jay's treaty was not renewed after the war of 1812–14. Even the peace-making amenities of 1815 failed to move British statesmen. Soon after the signing of the Treaty of Ghent a commercial convention was arranged by the two powers.[1] It was agreed (i) that there should be no discriminating duties in either country against the goods and vessels of the other, and no aggravating restrictions on shipping. (ii) The East India trade was opened to American ships, provided that they traded directly from the United States to the East Indies. The significant omission in the convention was that American vessels were forbidden general participation in the trade of the West Indies, although the West Indian planters and the American Government were both anxious for this concession. The Americans were very dissatisfied with the existing arrangement, for an English vessel could take a cargo from an English port to America and then go with a cargo of American goods to a British port in the West Indies which an American vessel could not enter. It might then load with sugar, rum, or molasses and either return to the United States for cotton or go directly home. This triangular trade was most valuable, and placed the American merchant carriers at a decided disadvantage. The interests of the West Indians were similarly injured by the exclusion of American vessels. Some years before, the West Indian planter, Brian Edwards, wrote, 'Under the present limited intercourse with America, the West Indies are subject to three sets of devouring monopolies: (i) the British ship-owners; (ii) their agents in American ports; (iii) their agents in the ports of the islands; all of whom exact an unnatural profit of the planters.'[2]

The impulse for reform became evident after the conclusion of peace in 1815. When the scourge of war was

[1] *Treaties and Conventions*, 344–7.

[2] Brian Edwards, *West Indies*, ii. 522, note (3 vols. 3rd ed., London, 1801).

past the need of putting the imperial house in order was generally recognized. Many voices proclaimed that a change was essential to adapt Britain's navigation and colonial system to the new world-wide conditions. In Parliament one of the first able champions of reform was Brougham. In March 1817 he made as thorough-going a free trade speech as any delivered in the later period, when the House of Commons was swayed by a phalanx of free traders.[1] He described the distressed state of the country, the falling off in shipping, the depression in manufactures, and attributed these conditions to two causes: the rapid transition from the conditions of war to those of peace and the protective system. His remedy was a fearless revision of the commercial code. Prohibition of imports had cut off supplies of iron and timber from the Baltic and thereby hampered the growth of industries and commerce. Removal of such prohibitions was expedient. Not merely fiscal arrangements but the navigation laws required a thorough overhauling. Brougham described the Navigation Act as having outlived its usefulness by a century:

> 'In our colonies it was enforced with unusual strictness—with what result? America said "since you will not suffer us to supply your settlements in any vessels but your own, we shall retaliate, and forthwith shut our ports against all vessels coming from ports from which you exclude ours". This was the substance of a Bill he held in his hand just passed by Congress.'[2]

Brougham did little more than express prevalent views. Significantly, Robinson, who answered him for the Government, freely admitted that protection was pernicious and that the only excuse for it was the infinite difficulty of escaping from it.[3] This critical attitude towards the commercial system was bred by the trade depression and the general slump in markets. For the relief of the situation so-called free traders had something positive to offer, and hence their creed found favour with those who shaped

[1] Hansard, 1st ser., 35. 1004.
[2] *Ibid.*
[3] *Ibid.* 1044.

British policy. The doctrines of Adam Smith were appealed to, but they would have exercised little magic influence had not the condition of trade demanded special treatment. Ample evidence of the advance of free trade ideas amongst parliamentarians is found in the debates of 1820. Baring presented to the House of Commons the famous petition of the merchants of London, and his introductory remarks were greeted with loud cheers from all sides of the House.[1] The burden of his speech was that the sole redemption from depression lay in a return to the principles of freedom. The modification of fiscal restrictions on the timber trade with the Scandinavian countries, the removal of prohibitive duties, and the abolition of the navigation laws were his suggestions for relief. The petition that he introduced laid down a precept for future action in the sentence 'that the maxim of buying in the cheapest market and selling in the dearest, which regulates every merchant in his individual dealings is strictly applicable as the best rule for the trade of the whole nation'. It concentrated its attack 'against every restrictive regulation of trade not essential to the revenue—against all duties merely protective from foreign competition—and against the excess of such duties as are partly for the purpose of revenue and partly for protection'.

In the ensuing discussion the principles of fiscal freedom were devoutly blessed by practically every section of the House. Lord Lansdowne in the House of Lords expounded the view that 'liberty of trade should be the rule and restraint only the exception'. Naturally the mercantile classes were more conservative than the parliamentarians in the adoption of the new principles. Those who had difficulty in finding markets for their products were zealous, but there was considerable lethargy and not a little fear that the newly suggested policy might bring injury to commercial interests. Tooke, who drew up the petition of the merchants of London, left on record that he had considerable difficulty in getting a sufficient number of signatures. But opinion in favour of change in the

[1] Hansard, 1st ser., I. 165. For the petition see 179–82.

old commercial system grew stronger, and was not confined to one side of the Atlantic. In the colonies protests were frequent against the navigation regulations as being injurious to colonial interests. In 1809 Sir Erasmus Gower, Governor of Newfoundland, reported discontent in that colony:

'It is eighteen years since I was first on this station, and the great improvements and changes that have taken place in that time render it now absolutely necessary that the capital of this colony should no longer be cramped, cabined and confined by laws and restrictions, which at present are entirely unsuited to its conditions and progress.'[1]

In the West India islands dissatisfaction with the Acts excluding American vessels was pronounced. Representative of such feeling was the petition in 1821 of the Legislative Council and General Assembly of Granada.[2] They claimed that the island was in great distress due to two causes. (i) The interruption of commerce with the United States 'by which we are prevented from receiving at moderate prices the productions of the States, and are deprived of an extensive market for our rum and molasses, which are readily received in barter for the supplies with which they furnished us'. (ii) The markets to which they were allowed access were impoverished. From 1783 it was the general aim of British statesmen that the West India islands should send their products, formerly marketed in the thirteen colonies, to the British provinces in the north, while the provinces in turn supplied the islands with timber and other commodities. But Granada complained that the northern colonies were unable to produce the material wanted, and that their produce could not be obtained on such favourable terms as that from the United States:

'In order, therefore, to grant the necessary relief and to remove our present distress and difficulties—we do humbly suggest that the ports of these islands should be generally thrown open for the admission of American vessels. In doing so, as matters are at present situated,

1 Prowse, D. W., *History of Newfoundland*, pp. 383–4 (London, 1895).
2 See report in *Montreal Gazette*, 16 January 1822.

little injury would be done to the trade and shipping of the United Kingdom. In the present restricted state of the American commerce, the greatest part of our supplies are conveyed a part of the voyage by their own vessels. It could therefore make but little difference to allow the Americans to come to our ports at once: and this would be more than compensated by our shipping being then permitted to trade direct to the States. We may add that the trade betwixt these islands and Nova Scotia and New Brunswick in native vessels is now nearly at an end; few of them come here, and we can place no dependence on any regular supply; this arises from their market being already overstocked with the produce they receive in exchange.'[1]

These views were frequently aired in other islands. In the northern continental colonies discontent with the navigation regulations was not so evident, although by no means absent. Nova Scotia and the two Canadas were chiefly concerned with getting a preference in the British market for their corn and timber. They condemned the imperial restrictions largely as an excuse to obtain such a preference. This fact was well illustrated in 1822 by the resolutions of the House of Assembly in Lower Canada, describing the restrictions on colonial trade as a severe grievance.[2] In 1819 the assembly and council of Nova Scotia appointed a special committee to investigate the trade of the province. The committee carefully interrogated leading merchants, and the consensus of opinion was strongly partial to reform. Upon the basis of their investigation the assembly resolved that 'it is immediately necessary that the colonies, in addition to the privileges they now enjoy, should be allowed the same freedom of trade with all the world which the people of the United States have acquired.'[3]

It was evident that by 1820 the old commercial and navigation system was ripe for reform. On both sides of the Atlantic opinion had swung in favour of adjustments to meet the new needs of empire in the nineteenth century.

[1] *Montreal Gazette*, 16 January 1822.

[2] *Journals of the House of Assembly for Lower Canada*, 2 Jan. 1822.

[3] See the anonymous pamphlet, *A General Description of Nova Scotia*. (Halifax, 1823), (Canadian Archives).

In 1820–1 a plan of campaign was outlined by parliamentary committees on foreign trade. In 1820 the committee of the House of Commons was under the able chairmanship of Wallace, Vice-President of the Board of Trade, with Huskisson as a prominent member. They showed the need of reform in a patchwork system, which by its very complexity perplexed merchants and depressed trade.[1] They considered that the modification of the navigation laws was essential, and suggested in particular that the prohibition contained in the great Navigation Act respecting Germany and the Netherlands might readily be removed. It was desirable to have every European state in amity with Great Britain on a footing of equal freedom. They also recommended modifications in the Act bearing upon trade with Asia, Africa, and America. The existing regulations, which prevented the importation of produce from Asia, Africa, and America directly in foreign vessels, necessitated much expense and delay, since such produce must be brought to a European port and thence in a British ship to England. The committee were frank in their profession of faith: 'They are convinced that every restriction on the freedom of commerce is in itself an evil, to be justified only by some adequate political expediency; and that every facility that can be extended to it is a benefit to the public interest.' Yet the old view that naval power rested on shipping regulations still lingered, and the committee refrained from recommending the complete abolition of the navigation laws.

In the succeeding year the discussions of 1820 were renewed. Wallace, pleading the commercial distress and the competition of other states, moved for another select committee. It was appointed, and dealt with the timber duties.[2] These duties were perhaps the most interesting example of colonial preference in the early nineteenth century. In 1809 they had been raised to the almost prohibitive amount of £3 5*s.* per load upon timber from

[1] See report, Hansard, 2nd ser., 5. appendix cxxx.

[2] Hansard, 2nd ser., 4. 425. See report Hansard, 2nd ser., 5. appendix xlix.

Europe, while that from British North America was admitted practically free. Such an arrangement was expected to serve a dual purpose: the development of an important colonial industry and the raising of revenue. Wallace's committee recommended the amendment of such duties, because Canadian timber was poorer than that of northern Europe, and the generous fiscal preference forced an article of inferior quality into consumption:

'The amount of the duty levied on Baltic timber and the increased price which under the operation of the duty, the American timber must have borne, may be considered as a bounty paid by the consumers of the United Kingdom for the benefit of the North American colonies and the support of the superfluous shipping in which the transport of their wood is said to afford the only employment.'

The preference was condemned as bad business. Yet the committee did not recommend its abolition. In a time of crisis the supply from northern Europe might fail, and British manufacturers suffer, if they were wholly dependent upon it. Encouragement for the colonial industry was essential to save Britain from dependence on foreign powers, and in addition some support to British shipping was necessary, even at the cost of uneconomical purchasing. Moreover, the vested interests in the American trade could not be abruptly sacrificed. Hence the committee concluded that the preferential duties should merely be reduced from £3 5*s*. per load to £2 5*s*. The reduction might be effected by taking 10*s*. from the duty on Baltic timber and imposing 10*s*. on that of colonial timber. After allowing for the ordinary difference in freight, this arrangement would leave a protection of 30*s*. per load in favour of the colonial product.

In the face of vigorous opposition from the shipping interests, Wallace incorporated such conclusions in an Act that has the prime significance of being the pioneer of those reforms which Huskisson effected.[1] Wallace rightly remarked that it was 'the first step in receding from a system detrimental to our commercial relations and towards conciliating those foreign powers without whose

[1] 1 and 2 Geo. IV, c. 37.

goodwill the relations of mercantile intercourse could never be securely established'.[1] It had two features that in the succeeding period are noticeable in most free trade legislation. (i) It was an attempt to build policy on what might be considered good business, irrespective of imperial sentiment. 'Buying in the cheapest market and selling in the dearest' was the cachet of the free trade creed in the twenties. It was a strictly utilitarian doctrine, although Huskisson, as we shall see, saved it from bleakness. (ii) It rested on the conviction that the ready marketing of British goods depended largely upon the conciliation of foreign states. By her fiscal freedom Britain would induce other states to follow her example, and thereby be able to push her manufactured products into their markets. International goodwill and national self-interest were strangely blended.

The spell of the old system was broken. After the changes in the timber duties, Robinson and Wallace, President and Vice-President of the Board of Trade, introduced sweeping reforms in the commercial and navigation regulations.[2] They were fitted into five Acts,[3] the Wallace-Robinson code, and constituted the basis for the later and more far-reaching measures of Huskisson and Robinson. The first repealed some 300 obsolete statutes regulating commerce, and dating from the reign of Edward III to the great Navigation Act, while the second dealt with statutes passed during and since the reign of Charles II, some of which it repealed and others it consolidated. Desecrating hands were placed upon the venerable Act of 1660. The important clauses three and four with other sections were repealed. The third clause read that 'no goods of the growth, product, or manufacture of Asia, Africa, or America shall be imported into England but in such ships as do truly belong to the English people, and are navigated by a master and three-fourths English mariners'. The fourth was to the effect that 'no goods or commodities

1 Hansard, 2nd ser., 6. 1500.

2 Wallace's speech, Hansard, 2nd ser., 7. 708.

3 3 Geo. IV, c. 41, 42, 43, 44, 45.

of foreign growth, production, or manufacture, which shall be brought into England otherwise than in ships built and navigated as above, shall be shipped from any other place but the place of their growth, production, or manufacture, or from those ports where they can only be or usually have been bought'.

Other statutes and parts of statutes from the reign of Charles II to 1822 were repealed, and the way was opened for a new Navigation Act, the third of Wallace's measures. (i) It allowed foreign ships to bring certain goods from any European port where they happened to be, provided that the ship belonged to the port in question. (ii) It permitted British ships to bring for later exportation the produce of Asia, Africa, and America from any place in Europe, instead of directly from the place of growth. The old rule had purposely required the long voyage in the belief that it bred hardier sailors. But if the goods were for use within England, and not for export, the old rule applied. (iii) It permitted goods of any country or place in America or the West Indies, which belonged or had belonged to Spain, to be imported direct from the place of growth in ships of the country. This provision was a bid for the trade of those independent Spanish territories no longer under the highly protective policy of Spain. They were thus put on much the same footing as the United States. (iv) Finally, the new Act placed Holland in precisely the same position as other European states. Since the Dutch had ceased to be formidable competitors there was no longer a reason for discrimination against them. The other two measures of the Wallace-Robinson code dealt with colonial trade. They extended the former relaxations, particularly those contained in the Act of 1805; for example, enumerated articles might be imported from foreign countries in North or South America into certain free trade ports in the British colonies, either in British vessels or the vessels of the country. This clause gave the concession in respect to West Indian trade long demanded by Americans and West Indians. In addition certain articles might be exported direct from such ports to foreign countries in

British or foreign vessels.[1] Also trade might be carried on from the British colonies direct to certain ports of Europe in British ships, instead of being shipped first to England.[2] But the commodities exported must be the growth, produce, or manufacture of the colonies. An Act already mentioned and passed during the Napoleonic war had permitted direct intercourse between certain colonial ports and Europe south of Finisterre. Wallace's measure extended this privilege. All of the leading British colonies in the western hemisphere were allowed at least one free port.

The significance of the Wallace-Robinson code is obvious, and was not hid from contemporaries. The *Annual Register* attributed to the Acts an importance 'vast beyond all question, not only from the direct effect of their enactments, but from the nature of the system of which they mark the commencement; this being the first instance in which practical statesmen have professed to act under the more liberal principles of political economy'. They were the foundation for the later laws of Huskisson and Robinson, and thus assisted in refashioning the complicated system of navigation regulations, the work largely of seventeenth-century statesmen, to the new conditions of the nineteenth century. They were adopted to remedy commercial distress. In the minds of men steeped in the newer political economy, wider markets for Britain's growing industries could emerge only through relaxation of the old system, and by 1822 wider markets were imperative.

These reforms synchronized with a reconstruction of the Liverpool ministry. In August 1822 Castlereagh committed suicide, and his place was taken by Canning. Peel already had gone to the Home Office. Vansittart found repose in the Lords, and Robinson succeeded him as Chancellor of the Exchequer, while in April 1823 Huskisson became President of the Board of Trade. This reshuffle of cabinet offices had instantly a favourable effect on reform. The Canningite wing acquired more influence in Tory

[1] 3 Geo. IV, c. 44, sections iii and iv.

[2] 3 Geo. IV, c. 45, sections ii and viii.

councils, and wielded it to promote the new policies. Above all, in Huskisson's hand was the opportunity to carry into effect his Liberal views on commercial matters. It was his good fortune to inherit the comprehensive achievements of Wallace and Robinson, and on their foundations he built. Without loss of time he grappled with the tasks before him.

One of his first measures was a Warehousing Bill to allow foreigners 'to deposit goods in British warehouses and take out for exportation without payment of duty'.[1] It was in harmony with the recommendation of the committee of 1820 that England should become a trade depot or grand emporium for the commerce of the world. In 1821 Wallace declared in a burst of enthusiasm that such policy would be a source of national wealth, greatness, and influence:

> 'To this cause might be attributed the opulence and prosperity of the commercial states of Italy in the middle ages. Those states possessed all the enterprise of commerce, and became the depot of the general produce of the world.... It certainly did appear to have been reserved for these days to see the policy of making this country the general depot of commerce.'[2]

In the old colonial system England was the staple for imperial trade. Goods were imported from the colonies and East Indies to be re-exported to European countries. In the eighteenth century a very large proportion of British exports to Europe represented this entrepôt trade. The new ideal in the nineteenth century, expressing a more cosmopolitan political economy and necessitated by the changes of 1822, was that she become an entrepôt for world trade.

A more notable measure was the Reciprocity Duties Bill. Since the passage of the great Navigation Act higher duties were imposed upon cargoes in foreign vessels than upon those imported in British bottoms, and in many instances smaller drawbacks were allowed upon articles exported in foreign than upon those exported in British ships. This policy as a means of promoting British shipping was justi-

[1] 4 Geo. IV, c. 24. This statute repealed or consolidated previous statutes on the subject.

[2] Hansard, 46. 1296–7.

fied so long as other nations acquiesced, but the United States adopted a retaliatory system. She imposed special duties upon all articles imported by British ships. Commerce between the two countries was embarrassed, and Britain was forced to place American vessels on the same footing as British. Portugal followed the example of the United States, and received the same treatment. Inevitably other states adopted retaliatory tactics. The Netherlands did so in 1821, and Prussia raised the duty on British ships and intimated further action unless changes were made in British policy. The British consul at Memel wrote that 'this difference between British and Prussian shipping . . . must drive the carrying trade in British bottoms from this port'.[1] Britain faced the alternative of commercial war or the relaxation of her old duties. How was she to meet the situation? She had now rivals who repudiated her terms. As M'Culloch wrote in the *Edinburgh Review*: 'Navigation laws and restrictive regulations are weapons we can no longer wield with success. We have taught others to use them with equal dexterity, and more effect. And a proper regard to our own self-interest is sufficient to show the advantage, or rather we should say, the necessity of reverting to a more just and liberal system.'[2] Huskisson, holding similar opinions, proposed that duties and drawbacks should be imposed and allowed upon all goods equally, whether carried in British or foreign vessels, giving the king in council a power to declare that such regulations should extend to all countries willing to grant reciprocal terms. But the power was reserved of maintaining the existing restrictions with respect to such states as should decline to reciprocate.[3]

'It was high time', he declared, 'in the improved state of the civilization of the world to establish new liberal principles, and to show that commerce was not the end but the means of diffusing comfort and enjoyment among the nations embarked in its pursuit. Those who had the largest trade must necessarily derive the greatest advantage from a better international regulation.'[4]

[1] *Speeches*, iii. 39.
[2] *Edinburgh Review*, May, 1823, p. 493.
[3] See 4 Geo. IV, c. 77.
[4] *Speeches*, ii. 205.

Like most of the early commercial reforms the Reciprocity Duties Bill was forced upon Britain by fear of damage to her far-flung trade, should continental states adopt the restrictive system. Out of necessity, not from altruism, she discarded the elements of protection. In defending the Reciprocity Duties Bill some years later Huskisson was emphatic in saying that 'if the system of discriminating duties for the encouragement of shipping were a secret known to this country alone; if a similar system were not, or could not be put in force in every country' the Bill would not have been passed.[1] The influence of the United States on British policy was pronounced. Her strong mercantile marine and the fact that she controlled roughly one-third of British export trade, gave her a weighty bargaining power. Largely out of a desire to conciliate her, Britain began the policy of relaxation. Yet the reservation under the Reciprocity Duties Bill to impose countervailing duties in case any foreign state imposed extra duties on the shipping of Britain was ironically first used against the United States. Notwithstanding the concessions to American vessels by the Wallace-Robinson Acts of 1822, the republican government continued an alien duty on the tonnage of British ships as well as on the cargo. Hence Britain retaliated, and the retaliatory policy was pursued by both sides till 1830.

In the years after 1823 most of the commercial states of both hemispheres negotiated with Britain reciprocity treaties, abolishing or equalizing discriminatory duties. These treaties or conventions frequently dealt broadly with commercial matters.[2] That with Denmark on 16 June 1824 was a type. It was the joint work of Huskisson and Canning. It stated that after a certain date Danish vessels on entering or departing from the ports of the United Kingdom should be subject to no higher duties than British vessels on entering or departing from such ports. The same rule applied conversely to British vessels entering or departing from the ports of Denmark. Pro-

[1] *Speeches*, iii. 29.

[2] See M'Culloch, *Dictionary of Commerce*, pp. 1404–76.

ducts of either country, imported or exported in its vessels, might likewise be exported or imported in the vessels of the other country. Products not of British growth or manufacture imported to Danish ports in British ships were subject only to such duties as products imported in Danish ships, and a similar provision pertained to produce imported in Danish ships to British ports. The convention was to be in force for ten years. The new policy was frequently criticized on the ground that in the duties no distinction was made between those countries whose ships were built at less expense than British vessels and those whose ships involved the same expense.[1] It was claimed that the British shipowner was thereby exposed to an unfair and injurious competition. But the reciprocity duties successfully weathered criticism from the press and within Parliament.[2]

Other reforms of Huskisson in his first year of office showed a similar attack on mercantilism. Such was the Scotch linen manufacture Bill, which removed restrictions on the linen industry of Scotland. Few measures were so expressive of early mercantile policy as an Act, containing forty sections, which meticulously regulated not only the bulk of the thread used but the length, breadth, and shape of the cloth manufactured.[3] This statute and others of like character were repealed. But of broader significance was the repeal of the Spitalfields Acts which concerned the most petted child of the protective system, the silk industry. Established in the fifteenth century the silk manufacture revealed no healthy development until the reign of Elizabeth, when the immigrant Huguenots gave it a powerful stimulus. In the seventeenth century its growth was appreciable. In 1666 there were no fewer than 40,000 persons employed by the trade. In its early history it was frequently protected by the prohibition of French and other imported silks, but until the end of the seventeenth century the protective measures were not rigidly enforced,

1 *Blackwood's*, September, 1828.

2 Hansard, 3rd ser., 24. 211, for debate on reciprocity duties in 1834.

3 13 Geo. I, c. 26.

and importation seems to have been generally free. But in 1697 the pressure of the silk interest made itself felt, and Parliament prohibited the importation of French and other European silk goods. In 1701 this prohibition was extended to the goods of India and China. Throughout the eighteenth century the industry in general was nursed by protection. From 1713 to 1765 heavy duties falling short of prohibition were imposed on manufactured silks, and from 1765 the import of such commodities was prohibited, and duties on other silks remained high. Under protection the industry grew, although in comparison with that of France it suffered from positive disadvantages, and had to compete with the smuggled goods of French manufacture.[1] It controlled a large part of the home market, and so influential were its champions in Parliament that in 1786 they forced Pitt to forgo his plan of extending the concession of the French commercial treaty to goods other than gauze, which the two contracting states agreed to admit at a 12 per cent. *ad valorem* duty.

The mercantilist regulations of this strong industry, Huskisson and his colleagues attacked. It was not the prohibitive duties with which Huskisson was at first concerned but the three Spitalfields Acts of 1773, 1792, and 1811. The French immigrant weavers had clustered in the neighbourhood of Spitalfields, which became the centre of the English industry. The normal weaver was a wage earner employed by a wealthy manufacturer with necessary capital. Inevitable friction over wages between employer and employee developed in the course of the eighteenth century, and resulted in frequent riots that necessitated the employment of the military. The first Spitalfields Act of 1773 was to prevent the recurrence of such troubles.[2] In a dispute between manufacturers and weavers it authorized the justices of Middlesex, Tower Hamlets, and the city to settle, regulate, and declare the wages of silk weavers in their respective areas. The masters who paid higher or

[1] See Hertz, G. B., 'The English Silk Industry in the eighteenth century' (*English Historical Review*, Oct., 1909, p. 720).

[2] 13 Geo. III, c. 68.

lower wages than those fixed were liable to a fine of £50. By the statute of 1792 [1] these provisions were extended to the manufacture of silk mixed with other materials, and by the later Act[2] magistrates were enabled to fix the wages of journeymen not hitherto included.

By such measures the weavers of Spitalfields became an aristocracy amongst wage earners. In cases of dispute with employers they usually received fair treatment from the magistrates.[3] Trade depressions might throw them out of work, but in general their condition was prosperous. Significantly in 1799 the ribbon workers of Warwickshire and the city and county of Coventry petitioned Parliament that they be brought under regulations similar to those of Spitalfields, complaining that many inconveniences resulted from the fact that there was 'no power of properly fixing, settling, and regulating the wages, pay, and price of the labour of the journeymen and work people'. As might be expected, employers had little sympathy with the Acts, and from the conclusion of peace in 1815 they condemned them as 'a relic of barbarism, an interference with capital and political economy, and a nursery of combination'.[4] The contemporary economists joined the chorus of denunciation. On the presentation of a petition of employers to Parliament in 1823 Ricardo expressed astonishment that such Acts were still on the statute book. 'They were not merely', he said, 'an interference with the freedom of trade but they cramped the freedom of labour itself.' [5]

In sympathy with such views, Huskisson in May 1823 discussed the Acts and intoduced a Repeal Bill. He admitted that they may have been defensible when the silk trade was confined to Spitalfields, but since silk manufacturing had spread elsewhere in England the only effect of the laws was to give undue advantages to the workers of a particular district.[6] In addition repeal would benefit the

[1] 32 Geo. III, c. 44 [2] 51 Geo. III, c. 7.

[3] See Hammond, J. L. and B., *The Skilled Labourer*, 213, and Clapham, J. H., 'The Spitalfields Acts 1773–1824' (*Economic Journal*, xxvi. p. 461).

[4] Petition of silk manufacturers to Parliament, May, 1823, Hansard, 2nd ser., 9. 143. [5] *Ibid.* 149. [6] *Speeches*, ii. 191.

industry in Spitalfields, for the employers had threatened to move elsewhere unless the law was altered. He considered it superfluous to appoint a committee of inquiry, since the Acts were an obvious evil. Fowell Buxton championed the cause of the weavers,[1] but Huskisson had the support of Ricardo, who argued that if the Acts were as good as described by Buxton, they should be applied to every trade indiscriminately.[2] He, however, was of the opinion that they were unsound, because they violated the principle that labour should be free. Notwithstanding a petition signed by 11,000 journeymen silk weavers of London and Middlesex protesting against any action, Huskisson piloted his Repeal Bill through the Commons, but in the Lords it was so badly mutilated that he dropped it. In the next year, practically the same Bill was carried safely through Commons and Lords, and the Spitalfields Acts which ran counter to the political economy of the age were removed. The effects of the repeal were variously judged. M'Culloch declared that the Acts had 'extinguished every germ of improvement' in the Spitalfields industry and had driven most of the valuable branches of the trade to Macclesfield, Manchester, Norwich, Paisley, and elsewhere. Their repeal in his estimation was the triumph of sound economics. But there is a reverse side to the picture. The later history of the weavers was one of melancholy distress, punctuated by strikes and disorders.[3] In 1834 two Spitalfields masters gave evidence before the select committee on hand-loom weavers and keenly regretted the repeal of the former Acts, as their distresses had been much greater since the repeal.[4] They suggested—an economic heresy in that age—a board of masters and workmen to regulate wages and fix a minimum. Liberals of Huskisson's school looked with scant sympathy upon anything like state regulation of economic life, and they readily and without reservation subjected the Spitalfields statutes to the axe. There was little else for them to do.

[1] Hansard, 2nd ser., 9. 810. [2] *Ibid.* 816.
[3] Hammond, J. L. and B., *The Skilled Labourer*, 219.
[4] Quoted, *Ibid.* 219–20.

In an age of rapid economic change adequate regulation was difficult. When a new industrial order had arisen the interference of the legislature would then be more possible and more defensible.

In the same year Huskisson dealt with a wider aspect of the silk trade. He and Robinson, Chancellor of the Exchequer, fashioned the first free trade budget of the century, with important consequences to the silk industry. At the opening of the year Robinson estimated that his sources of revenue would leave a surplus of £1,052,076, which added to that of the previous year would give a grand total of £2,763,061.[1] Looking to the end of 1827 he calculated on a surplus of £4,135,000, which would constitute a useful weapon for effecting fiscal reform. He and Huskisson therefore planned to reduce the duties on rum, coals, wool, and silk. The reduction of 6*d.* per lb. duty on foreign wool to 1*d.* and the liberty freely to export British wool on the payment of 1*d.* disclosed their audacity, but more significant were the fiscal arrangements respecting imported silks. Mercantilism produced no more pampered child than the silk industry, and an attack upon its privileges was substantial evidence of something new and bold in British policy. Since 1765 fully manufactured silks had been prohibited, and on other silks high duties were imposed. An *ad valorem* duty of 30 per cent. was now proposed instead of the former prohibition on such manufactured silks as shoes and gloves; on plain manufactured silks a duty of 15*s.* a lb.; on figured silk 20*s.* a lb.; and on other silks 30 per cent. *ad valorem*. On raw silks similar reductions were made. The duty on raw silk from the East Indies was reduced from 4*s.* to 3*d.* per lb.; on raw silk from China and Italy, from 5*s.* to 6*d.*, while the duty on organzine was brought down from 14*s.* 10*d.* to 7*s.* 6*d.* Such reductions enabled the home manufacturer to obtain raw material more cheaply.

Huskisson claimed that his proposals would wholesomely destroy the monopoly of the home producer: 'The system of monopoly in this trade has produced what mono-

[1] Hansard, 2nd ser., 5. 306.

poly is always sure to produce, an indifference with regard to improvement. That useful competition, which gives life to invention, which fosters ingenuity, and in manufacturing concerns promotes a desire to produce the article in the most economical form, has been completely extinguished. The system of prohibitory duties which has been maintained with respect to the silk trade has had the effect —to the shame of England be it spoken!—of leaving us far behind our neighbours in this branch of industry.' [1] By comparing the woollen and cotton industries he showed how the latter grew on a vaster scale largely because it was free from the protection and restrictions of the older industry. Freedom from legislative restraint bred independence and strength. Similarly the reduction of duties would revitalize the silk industry and enable it to compete successfully with that of the French. Moreover, the prohibitive system had evil social effects in that it encouraged smuggling and wholesale abuse of the law. In arguing that trade interests would benefit he expounded his own political creed and its justification in a characteristic passage:

'To be liberal in matters of commercial policy is to remove the difficulties and jealousies which have hitherto prevented a free intercourse between different nations, to extend to each the advantages and enjoyments of the other, and to promote arts, sciences, and civilization; and when we speak with reference to the commercial interests of this country, the argument is strengthened instead of being weakened. Her wealth, her industry, her talent, her prosperity, are so many inducements for us to liberalize the system. In short, sir, I would be liberal to other countries, because amongst other reasons, I feel that by being so, I best consult the interests of my own.' [2]

The new proposals met persistent opposition from the silk industry. Baring championed in the Commons the affected interests, and while agreeing that the reduction of the duty on the raw material was beneficial, considered that the lower duties on manufactured commodities was certainly evil.[3] The industry, he argued, could not stand

[1] *Speeches*, ii. 248. [2] *Ibid.*, ii. 258. [3] Hansard, 51. 732.

foreign competition, because (i) existing regulations between workmen and their masters hampered the industry; (ii) the price of food in England was double that in France; (iii) the French and Swiss obtained all their necessary raw material on better terms than did the English, since much of it was produced in France, and this fact rendered competition with them very difficult. Others supported Baring,[1] and petitions from the silk manufacturers accumulated. But Robinson disarmed the criticism of those in the industry by stating that 'he doubted much whether the measure would have been brought forward at all, if it depended upon the approbation of the silk manufacturers. Nearly all the persons in the trade were naturally hostile to the changes. But when the Government was about to negotiate on a broad principle, he thought it by no means necessary or proper, that they should negotiate with the parties immediately concerned.'[2] His words struck a significant note. The appeal to the 'broad principles' was an appeal to the teachings of Ricardian economics, which was the powerful undercurrent in the legislation of the period. The statesmanship that began with Pitt's careful perusal of Adam Smith was reaching fruition in the policy of Huskisson and Robinson.

The Government's proposals were carried, but to allow the industry to prepare for the change they did not become operative till 1826. James Deacon Hume, Controller of the Customs and later joint secretary to the Board of Trade, drafted the Bill,[3] and left on record the 'the intention of the Act of 1824 was to substitute a protecting duty of 30 per cent. in lieu of total prohibition'.[4] The silk manufacturers remained convinced that 30 per cent. was inadequate, and on the approach of July 1826, when the new duty was to come into force, agitated for its repeal. A motion by Ellice to refer the silk duties to a select committee gave Huskisson the opportunity to deliver one of his ablest speeches, and to build up a defence for his whole

[1] See Speech of Davenport, *ibid.* 737.

[2] *Ibid.* 1227.

[3] 5 Geo. IV, c. 21.

[4] *Report from Select Committee on the Silk Trade*, 1832, p. 5.

commercial policy, which was 'to unfetter the commerce of the country by the removal of those oppressive prohibitions and inconvenient restrictions, which had previously existed; and to give every facility and encouragement, consistent with vested interests, to the extension of the skill, the capital, and the industry of the people of England'.[1] He renewed his former arguments, particularly emphasizing that the removal of prohibitions on silk imports was necessary in view of the extensive smuggling. Prohibition failed to exclude French goods, and encouraged innumerable people to violate the law. The magnitude of smuggling might be roughly gauged by the fact that annually goods to the value of £100,000 were shipped from French ports to be smuggled into England. The percentage of such goods seized was very small. This situation alone seemed sufficient to condemn the prohibitive system.

What were the effects of Huskisson's policy on the silk industry? In the fifteen years after 1826 its influence was a subject of lively discussion. One need not enter deeply into the controversy, but it is necessary to make some attempt to discover to what extent Huskisson's expectations of benefiting British industry and abolishing smuggling were justified. In 1832 a select committee was appointed to discover the effects of Huskisson's enactments. It included prominent men, Sir Robert Peel, Joseph Hume, Poulett Thomson, Sir Henry Parnell, and Frankland Lewis. A mass of evidence covering nearly 1,000 pages was taken, but no report was made. Necessarily, the evidence was conflicting. Although it varied according to the interests of the witnesses, a few safe generalizations may be deduced from the ponderous mass of facts and personal observations.

The first obvious conclusion is that the majority of the silk manufacturers remained hostile to the new policy. They complained of inability to compete with the French, because the latter possessed greater natural advantages. Thomas F. Gibson of Spitalfields considered that the English manufacturer was not on an equality with the foreign producer, because (i) his raw material came from

[1] *Speeches*, ii. 470–1.

Italy and paid duty on entrance to England, while French manufacturers could readily obtain the raw material within the country. (ii) The French climate was more favourable to the silk industry. (iii) Labour in France was cheaper than in England. Gibson's evidence and views were supported by other witnesses of his class. A Mr. Brunskill estimated that in many lines of silk manufacture the cost in England was 30 per cent. greater than in France, while a ribbon manufacturer of Coventry went so far as to place it at 78 per cent. The economic historian is hardly in the position to verify such estimates. He can merely state them as opinions which influenced manufacturers in their hostility to Huskisson's fiscal reform. It is hardly necessary to point out that they would admit no improvement in the quality of British articles resulting from competition with France. They argued that the popular preference for French goods rendered nugatory any effort on their part to improve the character of their articles. One ribbon manufacturer remarked: 'Now there is no encouragement to improve; if we introduce ever so beautiful an article the French fashion is preferred, and our goods are considered as unsaleable and useless, if not exactly like theirs.' [1]

Witnesses who were not manufacturers told a different story. John Dillon, a warehouseman, considered that English goods had improved in quality since exposed to French competition, and a French manufacturer stated that he had never seen in the history of manufacturing an improvement so rapid as that in the English manufacture since 1826. In some articles, particularly in the coarser silks, the English industry had undoubtedly made improvements. In the finer fabrics it did little more than hold its own. 'In plain gros de Naples', Dillon remarked, 'the English have now almost, if not altogether, superseded the French.' [2] One of the best informed witnesses was Bowring, commercial commissioner at Paris. His evidence, backed by a mass of statistics, constituted the strongest defence of Huskisson's policy. In his reform Huskisson sought to strengthen the British industry in order that it

[1] *Report*, 84. [2] *Ibid.* 431.

might control to a larger extent the home market, and in addition capture a greater share of foreign trade. Bowring showed that the increased exports to France were convincing that the British industry had been greatly strengthened. He used the following table: [1]

Countries whence imported	*Quantities and value imported to France*					
	1828		1829		1830	
	Kil.	f.	Kil.	f.	Kil.	f.
England	1,087	119,570	3,507	385,770	5,852	643,720
Prussia	4,593	505,230	3,439	378,290	4,268	469,480
Other Countries	596	65,560	329	36,190	234	25,740
Totals	6,276	690,360	7,275	800,250	10,354	1,138,940

Other evidence strengthened Bowring's general conclusion. Even Brunskill admitted an immense increase in the manufacture of certain silks at Manchester, and a goodly portion of these went to France. Dillon, whose opinion as a warehouseman was valuable, recorded that the purchases of English silk goods since 1826 had considerably increased. [2] On one matter Huskisson's hopes remained unfulfilled. Smuggling had not decreased since 1826. J. D. Hume, at this time joint secretary to the Board of Trade and with no axe to grind, stated that since 1830 smuggling had increased. His remedy was the reduction of duties on manufactured silks from 30 per cent. to 25 per cent. which would remove the inducement to smuggle, as most purchasers preferred paying a 25 per cent. duty than buying from the smuggler while the cost of smuggling was 20 per cent. [3] Brunskill believed that smuggling had increased, and that the measures of 1824 operated as a license. His remedy, much different from Hume's, was prohibition. Huskisson's duty was either too low or too high. Had he been alive in 1832 he would probably have agreed with Hume.

[1] *Report*, 521. [2] *Ibid.* 430. [3] *Ibid.* 16.

The six years from 1826 to 1832 might seem an inadequate period to judge the effects of Huskisson's measures. Hence the evidence before the committee on import duties in 1840 has perhaps more weight than that in 1832. Many witnesses, especially Dillon, Hilton, Bowring, and Porter, attested to the steady growth of the industry from 1826 to 1840.[1] Porter's evidence was of particular importance, for he was head of the statistical department in the Board of Trade, and his statistics were above reproach. In his *Progress of the Nation* his figures illustrated the growth of the silk industry over a longer period, and are a more convincing proof than his evidence that Huskisson's measures were justified. Certainly the fears of manufacturers that the industry would be shattered by the changes of 1824 were ill founded. In the ten years preceding 1824 the quantity of raw and thrown silk used by British manufacturers amounted to 18,823,177 lb., or 1,882,311 lb. per annum. In the ten years immediately after that date the quantity used was 36,780,009 lb., or 3,678,001 lb. per annum, being an increase over the average of the former period of 95 per cent. In addition the export of British manufactured silks had increased, such increase being largely in the coarser grades:

Year	*Volume of exports*
1820	£371,755
1825	£296,736
1830	£321,010
1835	£972,031
1840	£792,648
1845	£766,405
1849	£998,334 [2]

There was no evidence of the decline of the silk industry under the fiscal arrangements of Robinson and Huskisson. On the contrary there was assurance of steady growth. But on the other hand smuggling did not decrease. A custom house statement illustrated that in the course of the seventeen years, 1827–43, 50 per cent. of the silk

[1] See *Report*, pp. 56, 92, 216–17, 191.
[2] Porter, *Progress of the Nation*, 219 (London, 1851).

goods shipped from France to Britain were smuggled.[1] So long as any trace of protection remained, the smuggler continued to ply his profitable trade. There was much force in M'Culloch's criticism of Huskisson's measure that a 15 per cent. duty on manufactured silks would have tended more amply to reduce smuggling than a 30 per cent. duty, because the latter was sufficiently high to make smuggling worth while.

The removal of the prohibitions on silk imports was an important attack on English mercantilism, but other measures with which Huskisson was associated were no less instrumental in freeing economic life from legislative restraints. Such was the repeal of the combination laws and the Acts of the previous century preventing the emigration of artisans and the exportation of tools and machinery. The Combination Act of 1799,[2] amended in 1800,[3] declared all existing and future combinations, contracts, and covenants among journeymen illegal and punishable, describing at great length the purposes of combination covered by the Act, such as combination to obtain advances of wages and to restrict the hours and quantity of work. The laws restricting the emigration of artisans were passed under George I,[4] and were extended by a statute in the reign of George III,[5] which stated that any person who should endeavour to entice a skilled artisan to leave England was liable to a considerable fine or to imprisonment, with heavy punishments for subsequent offences. Most of the laws against the exportation of machinery were also elaborated in George III's reign. A statute in 1774 stated that a person guilty of exporting tools or utensils used in the silk, cotton, linen, or woollen manufactures would forfeit the utensils and £200.[6] The captain of the ship must also forfeit £200. Other statutes increased the punishment.[7]

The classical economists from Adam Smith down were trenchant in their criticism of such legislation. M'Culloch

[1] Porter, *Progress of the Nation*, 223.
[2] 39 Geo. III, c. 81.
[3] 39 and 40 Geo. III, c. 106.
[4] 5 Geo. I, c. 27 and c. 28.
[5] 23 Geo. III, c. 13.
[6] 14 Geo. III, c. 71.
[7] 21 Geo. III, c. 37; 22 Geo. III, c. 60.

in the *Edinburgh Review* assailed the combination laws on the ground that they interfered with the sound principle that individuals should be free to sell their labour at whatever price seemed expedient to them.[1] A grievous restriction was placed on the liberty of workers when they were prevented from combining for the advancement of unduly low wages. Adam Smith's authority was invoked to support this argument. The combination laws were partial. They rested on the injustice of assisting one class against another. Workers were frequently punished for combination, but whatever might be the law employers managed to escape for a like offence. Similar arguments were used respecting the Acts against the emigration of artisans. They prevented the poor from bettering their lot in the United States. Emigration of impoverished artisans benefited both the country and the emigrants, since under prosperous conditions in America they could purchase and consume more British goods than in England, and also save the mother-land the expense of their upkeep. The laws prohibiting the exportation of machinery were similarly indefensible. They forced foreigners to construct machines for themselves, and thus become rivals of British industry. From 1814 Francis Place with tireless energy and consummate ingenuity worked for the repeal of the combination laws, and largely under his influence Joseph Hume championed it in Parliament. In February 1824 Hume moved for a committee to investigate the Acts respecting the emigration of artisans, the exportation of tools and machinery, and combinations.[2] Huskisson enthusiastically seconded the motion, although according to Francis Place, he was not at first very sympathetic towards the removal of the combination laws.[3] He condemned prohibitions on the emigration of artisans on the ground that 'every man was entitled to carry that talent which nature had given him, and those acquirements which his diligence had attained,

1 *Edinburgh Review*, January, 1824.

2 Hansard, 2nd ser., 10. 141.

3 See Place's story of the repeal of the combination laws in his Life by Graham Wallas, chapter viii. (London, 1918).

to any market in which he was likely to obtain the highest remuneration; unless it could be shown that there was some paramount and overwhelming necessity against it'.[1] Of the combination laws he said that they 'had greatly aggravated the evil they were intended to remove', for combinations had increased instead of diminished.

The committee was appointed, with Hume as Chairman and Huskisson a member but an irregular attendant. Hume, assisted by the lobbying genius of Place, obtained an abundance of evidence in favour of the trade union case, and in the spirit of contemporary political economy the committee condemned the combination laws. They recommended that masters and workmen be freed from such restrictions as regards the rate of wages and the hours of working, but that the laws regulating the settlement of disputes by arbitration between masters and workmen be consolidated and made applicable to all trades.[2] They also advocated repeal of the laws that prevented artisans from going abroad, and asked for time to investigate more fully those dealing with the exportation of machinery. With little delay Bills were introduced repealing the laws against combinations and the emigration of skilled workmen.[3]

But the last word was not heard of the combination laws. It was a period of labour unrest, and repeal of the Acts tended to accentuate it. Unions rapidly developed with aims destructive of industrial peace. In great alarm employers throughout the country petitioned the Government to have the old laws re-enacted. The shipowners of Liverpool appealed to Huskisson, and used all the pressure of which they were capable to induce him to pass repressive measures against the workmen. At first he was prepared to let the Act of the former year remain, but in the spring of 1825 he came to share the alarm of others in the Government, and earned the dislike of both Place and Hume by moving for a select committee to inquire into the effect of the Act of the previous year. In his speech, which according to Place 'drew a false and exaggerated

[1] *Speeches*, ii. 221.

[2] Hansard, N.S. 11. 811.

[3] 5 Geo. IV, c. 95, c. 97.

picture of the state of the country', he assumed blame for inattention to the business of the former committee and for not having scrutinized Hume's Acts.[1] The consequence was that all statutes relative to combinations and conspiracies of workmen were repealed, and there was no means of applying a legal remedy to the industrial disorder. Unions intimidated workmen and employees, and laid down regulations for those who were not even members. Such a situation upset Huskisson's confidence in the measures which he himself had sponsored. He believed that it was the function of the State to hold carefully the balance between capital and labour, and to allow free bargaining to both. But free bargaining was endangered by the aims of many of the working-men's combinations. He cited the case of one organization in which no member was at liberty to engage himself for any given time or price without the consent of the committee of management. The seaman's union had determined not to submit to the authority of any persons whom they had not appointed or approved. In view of such facts Huskisson considered a committee necessary to take a new survey of the subject. The committee was appointed, with a carefully selected membership, and under the chairmanship of Wallace recommended that all associations be considered illegal except those for the purpose of settling collectively the amount of wages and the hours of work. Associations for the purpose of intimidating men to leave work or join a combination were to be illegal. A Bill on these conclusions was carried, and the right of collective bargaining was thus recognized by early nineteenth-century Liberalism.[2]

Readers of Place's life know how bitterly he criticized Huskisson for reconsidering the Act of 1824. He described him as mean, deceitful, hypocritical, and wholly swayed by the wealthy shipowners of Liverpool. However, as Place used similar abusive terms of almost all the ministers of the time—Peel he disposed of as 'a pitiful shuffling fellow'—his censure loses some of its weight, unless we

[1] *Speeches*, ii. 362. See a very full report of his speech, *Annual Register*, 1825.

[2] 6 Geo. IV, c. 129.

accept the cynical conclusion that the statesmen of the period were all rascals. In the nature of things Place could have little sympathy with Huskisson. He was a Radical who had spent many laborious years working for the repeal of the combination laws, and was naturally irritated when Huskisson seemed to hesitate in performing the great work. The foremost aim of his life was the laudable one of obtaining relief for the workers. Huskisson's mind, on the contrary, was absorbed by consideration of those policies which would promote British trade and industrial power. He was neither a social reformer nor a Radical, and hence he laid less emphasis upon Place's pet project, repeal of the combination laws, than upon other policies. Place's criticism of Huskisson was a case of the kettle criticizing the pot for not being a kettle. Moreover, we need not doubt the sincerity of Huskisson's arguments for repeal of the combination laws. He was in favour of repeal, and his attitude on the subject was in harmony with his general Liberalism.

V

THE GREAT REFORMS

THE changes considered in the previous chapter in the old commercial system were merely heralds to greater inroads into mercantile theory. In 1825 Robinson and Huskisson made changes for which the previous reforms were only preliminary. Not for seventeen years were such deep fissures to be opened in fiscal and commercial arrangements, and Peel's experiments in 1842–6 were elaborately prefaced by those of Huskisson in 1825. The basic principle of these measures was that so frequently invoked since 1821, freedom. Liberty from the many restraints of parliamentary Acts was the central strand in the new policy. It was accepted by Great Britain out of the necessity to break down protection in Europe, in order to have a readier market for the accumulating output of her industries. It was the lusty call of self-interest that directed her to open the doors of her home markets. Her commercial and industrial power no longer rested on national protection. Her industries had grown to vigorous manhood. They no longer feared rivals, for they were robust enough to be confident of victory in any competition. Their imperative need was wider markets attained through freedom of exchange with other states. Without this, Britain's early industrialization was valueless, because her industries could not grow. They were strong, but they could not become stronger without more room to expand. Hence under the guidance of Huskisson and Robinson, Britain endeavoured to set the pace in the relaxation of commercial regulations.

The measures of 1825 constituted a threefold attack on the old system: (i) Considerable changes were effected in the prohibitions and high protective duties, and, as a corollary, the existing customs were consolidated. (ii) Radical alterations were made in the Navigation Acts with the object of removing those provisions which tended to make the colonies little more than economic supplements of the mother-state. (iii) There was a bold reform of shipping regulations and discriminations, many of which had conformed to no principle and were objectionable in that they handicapped shipping.

The pruning of the protectionist tariff claims first attention. The existing customs schedule was the child of a long past. Since the Restoration duties had been imposed, increased, and amended in such a manner as to render the tariff a monument of complexity. In 1815 there were 1,100 Customs Acts in force, and additions were made in the succeeding ten years.[1] The financial exigencies of previous governments and the desire to protect domestic industries were the principal explanations for this unwieldy mass of legislation. Its cumulative effect was that a duty for protection or revenue fell on almost every conceivable article of import. To assess and collect these numerous duties, custom houses were scattered in every part of the kingdom, even in the smallest and most distant fishing hamlets, and the consequent expenses necessarily devoured much of the revenue. In many cases where revenue was the object, the duties were so high as to limit the import of the articles, and hence to reduce the total return. In other cases prohibitions and restrictions were maintained, although by 1825 the reason for the restrictions had long ceased to operate. A famous report on customs tariffs states that:

'ever since the year 1660, a positive prohibition has existed, and been enforced, against the importation from the Netherlands and Germany, in any ships whatever, of wines, spices, groceries, almonds, currants, dates, ginger, liquorice, pepper, raisins, figs, prunes, sugar, tobacco, potashes, pitch, tar, salt, rosin, timber, olive oil, and numerous other articles. This legislation had originally taken its rise in the old maritime rivalry of the country with the Dutch, especially in the carriage of East Indian produce, and it had been fostered in consequence of the monopoly of the eastern trade possessed by the East India Company, whose privilege of exclusive trade would have

[1] See *Customs Tariffs of the United Kingdom*, 1800–97 (Imperial Bluebook), 38.

been worthless if so enterprising a nation as the Dutch, whose warehouses lay at our very doors, could have imported goods from countries whose trade was absolutely closed, even to British subjects, except by the license of the company.'[1]

Other abuses clung like ivy to tariff regulations. Their nature is best seen in Huskisson's explanations for the projected changes. The abuses were so obvious to him and Robinson that at the opening of the year they concentrated attention on them.

Robinson in his budget of February 1825 made the first step in reform.[2] To cover any diminution in revenue due to the reduction of duties he sought an adequate surplus. With the glowing optimism that earned him the epithet 'Prosperity Robinson', he explained that for 1824 he had calculated on a surplus of £420,000. His hopes had been more than fulfilled, for he obtained £1,437,744. His financial plans were floated at a fortunate period. A pronounced trade boom was in progress, and assisted him greatly. With zeal warmed by such a satisfactory return from his first free trade budget, he resolved on deeper fiscal changes. He calculated that for the year 1825 his expenditure would amount to £56,001,842 and his revenue to £56,445,370, leaving him a surplus of £443,528. For the year 1826 he looked to a surplus of £864,676 and for 1827, £1,254,676. These surpluses he intended to use for the encouragement of home consumption, the extension of British commerce abroad, the restriction of smuggling, and some slight alleviation in the pressure of direct taxation. Such a fourfold objective was sought through the reduction of duties. As the majority of duties were of a protective rather than of a revenue character, the determination of the new duties was left to Huskisson, whose department was responsible for that subject. Robinson's task was to safeguard a sufficient revenue; Huskisson's, to rejuvenate industry. Robinson was, therefore, content in February merely to outline broadly the fiscal programme and to mention the reductions on revenue duties.

1 *Customs Tariffs of the United Kingdom*, 38.

2 Hansard, N.S. 12. 719.

On 25 March Huskisson laid before Parliament his comprehensive plan for revitalizing industry through fiscal change.[1] He directed attention first to the cotton manufactures in which British supremacy was pronounced. Notwithstanding that in this industry Britain had no dangerous competitor, the duties were high. On a certain description of cotton goods they were 75 per cent.; on another, 67 per cent.; on a third, 50 per cent. The gradation of duties was intended to benefit the British manufacturer in the various kinds of cottons, but Huskisson swept aside 'these absurd duties, and equally absurd distinctions', and fixed on the uniform duty of 10 per cent. as 'sufficient to countervail the small duty levied upon the importation of the raw material into this country, and the duty upon any other articles used in the manufacture'. A higher duty he considered mischievous, for it would make the home producer too conscious of his monopoly.

The woollen manufacture was the oldest and one of the most petted children of mercantilism, but Huskisson was determined to expose it to the rigorous forces of competition, believing that like most favourites it had 'suffered rather than profited, by being spoiled and petted in rearing'. He pointed out that although it had been more favoured by the legislature than the cotton industry, yet its development since 1765 had lagged far behind its younger and ill-favoured competitor. The following are briefly the facts on which Huskisson based his conclusions:

	1765	1825
Quantity of cotton wool imported in year ending 5th January.	3,360,000 lb.	147,174,000 lb.
Value of cotton goods exported in year ending 5th January	£20,000	£30,795,000
Quantity of lambs' and sheeps' wool imported in year ending 5th Jan.	1,926,000 lb.	23,858,000 lb.
Value of woollen goods exported in year ending 5th January.	£5,159,000	£6,926,000[2]

The dilatory growth of the woollen industry in contrast to the rapid growth of the cotton did not speak favourably

[1] *Speeches*, ii. 327.

[2] *Ibid.*, ii. 332.

for the value of legislative nurturing. Huskisson concluded that 'prosperity will be most effectually promoted by an unrestrained competition, not only between the capital and industry of different classes in the same country, but also by extending that competition as much as possible to all other countries'. The existing duties on woollen manufactures varied from £67 10*s.* to £50 per cent. He was satisfied that a duty of £15 would give adequate protection and introduce a health-giving competition to British manufactures.

The linen industry was also the victim of excessive nursing. The existing duties fluctuated from £40 to £180 per cent. Huskisson reduced all of them to £25 per cent. Printed books, bound, paid £6 10*s.* the cwt.; unbound, £5. He reduced them to £3 10*s.* and £3 respectively. The £80 per cent. on glass was reduced to £20 per cent. Similar changes were made on other articles. Huskisson laid special emphasis upon the reductions on iron. Raw iron was a feeder to such industries as the manufacture of hardware, and the duty of £6 10*s.* a ton constituted a restraint on their development. Swedish iron, considered superior to the British, was procurable at lower prices, and only the existing duty prevented the British manufacturer from using it. The reduction of the duty on raw iron would benefit the secondary stages of the British industry, and was the more urgently required in that the produce of the British mines was not adequate for the home demand. Huskisson proposed to cut the duty to £1 10*s.* a ton. Raw copper was in the same category as raw iron. The existing duty was £54 a ton, which tended to check the British manufacturer from obtaining raw copper abroad. Huskisson was emphatic that 'if the price of our copper manufactures is to exceed that of the like articles of foreign manufacture, in anything like a proportion to this enormous duty, it is evident, that even assuming some superiority in the skill of our workmen, we must ultimately be driven from the markets of other countries.'[1] He proposed to reduce the duty from £54 to £27 a ton. A similar fate

[1] *Ibid.*, ii. 338.

befell the imposts on other metals. The duty on foreign zinc was reduced from £28 a ton to £14 a ton; that on tin, from £5 9*s*. 3*d*. to £2 10*s*. the cwt.; that on lead, from £20 per cent. *ad valorem* to £15, which Huskisson hoped would be 'sufficient to admit of a foreign import, and to check the present exorbitant price of that metal'.

He dealt with non-enumerated articles by an omnibus clause. Under the existing customs rates, all non-enumerated manufactured articles paid 50 per cent. of their estimated value; those unmanufactured, 20 per cent. The system frequently proved burdensome to importers. There was the surprising case of the gentleman who imported a mummy from Egypt. The customs officers, puzzled whether to consider it a raw product or a manufactured article, finally categorized it as a manufactured article and imposed a duty of £200, or 50 per cent. of its declared value. Under Huskisson's omnibus clause the duty on manufactured articles, not enumerated, was reduced from 50 per cent. to 20 per cent. and on articles unmanufactured from 20 per cent. to 10 per cent. Huskisson's guiding principle was that where the duty existed for protection and not for revenue, it should in no case exceed 30 per cent:

'If the article be not manufactured much cheaper or much better abroad than at home, such a duty is ample for protection. If it be manufactured so much cheaper, or so much better abroad, as to render 30 per cent. insufficient, my answer is, first, that a greater protection is only a premium to the smuggler; and secondly, that there is no wisdom in attempting to bolster up a competition, which this degree of protection will not sustain. Let the state have the tax, which is now the reward of the smuggler, and let the consumer have the better and cheaper article, without the painful consciousness that he is consulting his own convenience at the expense of daily violating the laws of his country.' [1]

Huskisson's general programme outlined in March was accompanied by a schedule of reduced duties upon raw material necessary for manufacturing; such as dye pro-

[1] *Speeches*, ii. 342.

ducts, olive oil, oil from rape seed, and wool. In the following months he heard deputations from the interests affected by the proposed changes, and made slight alterations in his original schedule. He lowered the duty on lead, suggested a different mode of levying the duty on linen manufactures and glass, and modified his former duty on books and manuscript. The new schedules were accompanied by a thorough consolidation and simplification of the customs regulations.[1] This latter was the work of a man whom Huskisson consulted through the whole course of his labours, James Deacon Hume, Controller of the Customs.

In modern arguments for a low tariff emphasis is generally laid upon the benefit to the consumer. A distinction is frequently made between his interests and those of the producer. It is presumed that his interests are served by free trade; those of the producer by protection. Huskisson repudiated such distinctions. His argument for fiscal change were three: (i) removal of prohibitions and reduction of duties would benefit concurrently consumers and producers; (ii) it would remove a social evil, smuggling; (iii) it would set an example to other states, and by lessening the merciless competition of tariffs go far to bring about international harmony. The removal of prohibitions and high duties benefited the producer, because it provided him with the essential stimulus of competition. It urged him to strengthen and perfect his own manufacture, and if necessary to remodel his methods to hold his own in the exacting contest with foreign rivals. Prohibition, by giving a monopoly to the home producer, was a premium to mediocrity, and destroyed the best incentive of excellence, while it exposed the consumer to rapid and inconvenient fluctuations of price, and forced him to trade with the smuggler for those articles which his taste might prefer. Furthermore, prohibition notoriously failed in its object. It did not exclude foreign goods, which freely entered through the illicit channel of smuggling. Smuggling had become an evil of gigantic proportions.

[1] See the Acts: 6 Geo. IV, c. 104; 6 Geo. IV, c. 105; 6 Geo. IV, c. 106; 6 Geo. IV, c. 111.

'Its active instruments', declared Robinson in a burst of parliamentary indignation, 'haunt us wherever we go; they hover round our coast, they penetrate our harbours, they traverse the interior; they invade the splendid palace of the noble, and the humble cottage of the poor; they offer their temptations in every quarter, and I fear that all classes of society yield to the seduction.' [1]

Huskisson spoke of the smugglers training their children 'in a state of perpetual warfare with the law, till they insensibly acquire the habits and feeling of outlaws, standing rather in the relation of pirates, than of fellow-subjects, to the rest of the community'.[2] Removal of prohibitions and reduction of duties seemed the only reliable means of remedying such a social disease, and would, in his eyes, almost alone justify fiscal change.

The Manchester Liberals in the next decade pleaded in the eloquent voice and powerful pen of Richard Cobden that commercial restrictions and prohibitive tariffs were the prime source of international strife, and that the healing of the nations could come only through a destruction of the restraints upon trade. In their creed, trade was an infallible salve for national animosities. That view is evident, although sketched in less bold outline, in Huskisson's arguments for the removal of prohibitions. A freer trade would help to attain a better world economy, ever an active ideal of his political speculations. Conscious that there was little enthusiasm amongst continental statesmen for the principles of fiscal freedom he none the less believed that

'when the governments of the continent shall have contemplated, for a few years longer, the happy consequences of the system in which we are now proceeding, that their eyes will be opened. They will then believe—but, at present they do not—that we are sincere and consistent in our principles; and, for their own advantage, they will then imitate us in our present course, as they have, of late, been adopting our cast-off system of restrictions and prohibitions.' [3]

This optimistic faith later found more forcible expression

[1] Hansard, 2nd ser., 12. 734.

[2] *Speeches*, ii. 343.

[3] *Ibid.*, ii. 349.

in the speeches of the Cobdenites. Like them Huskisson would not retard fiscal change until foreign states accepted the new principles. But to hasten European countries in the adoption of a free trade policy in reciprocal agreements with Britain he suggested the addition of one-fifth to the proposed duties upon the productions of those countries which might refuse to place British commerce and navigation upon the footing of the most favoured nation. In the spirit of Adam Smith he did not shrink from using the tariff as a temporary means to attain a freer trade, which he was convinced would harmonize relations amongst the great states. One need not examine where Huskisson placed the emphasis; whether on the international good of the new fiscal principles or on the national interest. He saw no contradiction between the two; the one policy served both.

The limited nature of Huskisson's tariff reform is apparent. He accepted as whole heartedly as Peel did later the free trade doctrine, but in its application he was hampered by a number of factors, the most pronounced of which were his party affiliations. He and his associates had to educate both their own party and Parliament. An attempt to effect sweeping changes would merely have stiffened the resistance of the opposition, and perhaps have postponed reform indefinitely. Furthermore, Huskisson believed that in economic policy gradual change was far the soundest. It allowed the interests affected to readjust their position to the new policy, and it avoided the lacerating effects of revolutionary measures. Hence he defended moderate protection. In addition he wished to test European competition. Whenever he discovered that British industries had little to fear from continental rivals he would reduce further the duties on the foreign articles. He thereby fully earned the criticism of List that he 'followed pretty much the rules of the Dutch water administration. Wherever the water on the outside rises high, these wise authorities erect high dykes; wherever it rises less, they only build lower dykes. After such a fashion the reform of the English commercial policy which was announced with so much pomp reduced itself to a piece of mere politico-economical jugglery.' [1]

Indeed Huskisson might be accused of slowness in lowering the dykes, when there was little danger from the rising flood. The duties on woollen and cotton manufactures afford an illustration. Although in these industries the British manufacturers had no formidable rivals, he maintained a duty of 15 per cent. on woollens and 10 per cent. on cottons. Parnell, whole hearted in his acceptance of free trade principles, argued that there was no justification for such duties. The British woollen industry had a predominant superiority over foreign competitors. The 15 per cent. duty on earthenware came under the same criticism, for in this industry Britain was considerably in advance of other states. For a different reason Parnell criticized the 25 per cent. on linens. It amounted to a prohibition, and its only effect would be to postpone the introduction of new machinery in the British industry. The duty of 50 per cent. on beads, pomatum, skates, and tooth-powder was irksome to the public, and the 100 per cent. on currants and oranges was objectionable in that it fell on the industrious middle classes. Such schedules in Parnell's judgement, were at variance with the general principles of open competition laid down by the President of the Board of Trade.[2]

In full justice to Huskisson it should be said that his chief aim was the removal of prohibitions and prohibitive duties, not the abolition of protection, and in respect to the major industries of Britain his new tariff schedules succeeded. Yet the removal of prohibitions was perhaps inadequate. Under the circumstances, further tariff pruning might have benefited the home producer and consumer, and would certainly have increased the revenue. Parnell in his *Financial Reform* pointed out that comparatively few articles produced the greater portion of the revenue. It appeared from accounts laid before the committee of finance that in 1827 the revenue from the cus-

[1] List, F., *National System of Political Economy*, 372 (London, 1885).

[2] Hansard 2nd ser., 13. 1222.

toms' duties was reaped from 566 duties on as many different articles:

18 articles produced	£17,683,445 8*s.* 8*d.* out of a gross revenue of £19,815,206 3*s.* 1½*d.* or £100,000 for each article.
9 articles produced	£784,415 18*s.* 6*d.* or £50,000 to £100,000 for each.
9 articles produced	£370,066 17*s.* 1*d.* or £25,000 to £50,000 for each.
20 articles produced	£370,402 5*s.* 1*d.* or £10,000 to £25,000 for each.
510 articles produced	£585,072 6*s.* 0*d.* or less than £10,000 for each.
Miscellaneous articles produced	£20,903 7*s.* 7*d.*[1]

The committee on import duties in 1840 found the tariff much as Huskisson left it, and were not ambiguous in their criticism. They claimed that 'the tariff of the United Kingdom presents neither congruity nor unity of purpose; no general principles seem to have been applied', and they pointed out that 17 articles produced 94½ per cent. of the revenue. Huskisson might have reduced duties on hundreds of articles with gain to the revenue, and probably with wholesome results to home production. Every article with a return of less than £10,000 needlessly rendered a delay and loss in the collection of customs, and the abolition of duties on such articles would have been sound economy. An examination of Huskisson's opinions affords conclusive proof that in theory at least he was favourable to the removal of such duties: 'By acting on the principles of free trade, I understand that we ought to lessen or remove every restriction on our commerce that tends to cramp the energies of individual enterprise, without benefiting the revenue.'[2] He was restrained from further action in 1825 not so much by blindness to the condition of the tariff as by the strength of vested interests

1 Parnell, H., *Financial Reform*, 114 (3rd ed., London, 1831).

2 *Speeches*, iii. 421.

and the force of conservative opinion within his party. He was compelled to await the future for an opportunity to give his ideas expression.

Tariff revision was less important than another reform by Huskisson in the same year, the reshaping of the navigation system through the destruction of the monopoly hitherto exercised by the mother-country over colonial trade. In this matter he revealed a bold constructiveness in dealing with a system long sacred to British political thinkers, and he gave evidence of a liberal imperialism new to British statesmen. The magnitude of Huskisson's conceptions will be best realized when it is pointed out that in the twenties a mood of pessimism on the value and future of colonial possessions dominated British thought. The American Revolution was gloomily interpreted as proof that the destiny of colonies was separation. It was merely a matter of time until the Empire's existing colonial territories followed the path of those communities which constituted the United States. In addition there was a prevalent opinion that colonies were an economic loss. On the occasion of the modification of the Canadian timber duties in 1822 Sir Isaac Coffin declared that

'it would have been a good thing for this country if Canada had been sunk to the bottom of the sea; it cost us £500,000 per annum and did not make a return of 500 pence. It had been cheating this country out of £300,000 a year by suffering great quantities of American timber to be sent down the St. Lawrence and brought to England as Canadian.... The sooner the Governor was called home, and the assembly and colony suffered to go to the devil, the better.' [1]

In 1825, on the eve of the introduction of Huskisson's new programme, Baring expressed the discontent of many parliamentarians over the burden of the colonies in his statement that 'he would recommend to the Government to call on the legislature of Canada to enquire whether they felt themselves strong enough to separate from the mother country'.[2] A few days later Captain Moberly ventured the remark that the sooner Britain got rid of the West Indies the better for her interests. Looked at from the

[1] Hansard, 2nd ser., 6. 1073.

[2] *Ibid.* 12. 1033.

point of view of a cash nexus, the Empire to the utilitarian thinkers of the twenties was a union in which they could see neither logic nor purpose. The test of value was the test of tangible profits; and since Britain's second Empire could not produce a convincing balance sheet, no reasons were apparent for perpetuating a meaningless political scheme.

Of course such pessimism did not entirely represent British opinion on the subject of colonies. Alongside of it should be placed the verdict of such men as Alexander Macdonell who in 1828 attempted to vindicate the maintenance of colonies.[1] They 'are eminently beneficial and contribute to the prosperity and maritime strength of this kingdom'. Yet on the whole imperial vision in the twenties had grown feeble, and it was in an atmosphere of indifference, if not of hostility, to Britain's oversea possessions that Huskisson on 21 March rose to explain reforms intended to unite 'the mutual interests and draw closer the bonds of harmony and good understanding' between the mother-state and her dependencies. Huskisson's policy rested on the conviction that the old colonial system had failed and must in the future more lamentably fail to meet the needs of Empire. Evidences of its past failure were the unhappy state of Ireland and the American Revolution for which 'the train had been long laid in the severe and exasperating efforts of this country to enforce with inopportune and increasing vigour, the strictest and most annoying regulations of our colonial and navigation code'.[2] In Ireland and the American colonies the policy of subordinating the economic interests of the dependency to those of Britain had been pursued with the same fatal consequences to harmonious relationships. Significantly, Huskisson's policy was shaped by his interpretation of the American Revolution. Few of the prominent British contemporaries of that movement had considered the revolution as in any way due to the economic regulations of the old colonial system. Burke, for example, took pains to point out that the Americans did not rebel against the

[1] *Colonial Commerce* (London, 1828). [2] *Speeches*, iii. 10.

restraints of the commercial system which had grown with their growth and strengthened with their strength. But Huskisson interpreted the revolution as the inexorable child of the restrictions on colonial trade, and he was prepared to utilize this explanation as a powerful reason for the modification of those restrictions.

The old system was condemned not only by the past. A new political world had emerged from the shocks of the revolutionary period, and its existence made it clear that Britain could not advantageously monopolize the trade of her colonies. The extensive South American territories, hitherto under Spain and Portugal, were independent, and anxious for trade with Europe and North America. As these countries absorbed the trade of the western hemisphere, the colonies, the shipping, and the commerce of Britain must suffer. The policy that would alone promote British interests was that of opening direct trade between the colonies and other countries in Europe and America. Such was Huskisson's aim; and to it the grinding necessities of the new international situation lent emphatic support. What the Wallace-Robinson code had begun, he completed.

Although Huskisson sought to liberate the colonies from the restraints of the navigation laws, he did not wish to loosen the political connexion. He expected that the new arrangements would preserve to the colonies and the mother country 'all the commercial benefits of a free trade, together with all the political advantages of our continuing parts of one great empire, and enjoying alike, under the sway and protection of the same sovereign, all the rights and privileges of British subjects'.[1] His policy aimed to remove from the existing Empire the prohibitions of a system, evolved in the seventeenth century to fit apparent seventeenth-century needs, but lamentably out of harmony with the requirements of the newer Britain and her dominions. He proposed to open the export and import commerce of the colonies to all states prepared to reciprocate, practically on the same principle on which they were at

[1] *Speeches*, ii. 313.

liberty to trade with Jersey or with Ireland. The old enumeration list was to be discarded, and with the exception of some articles—such as fire-arms, ammunition of war generally, sugar, rum, and salted fish—there was to be free intercourse between British colonies and reciprocating countries, either in British ships or in ships of those countries. The Wallace-Robinson code had allowed such trade between the British colonies and the states in the western hemisphere. Huskisson now extended the freedom to the trade of the colonies with European states. Intercourse was to be carried on through specified ports, and to be subject to duties fixed by British statutes.[1] In the next twenty-four years, seventeen countries made treaties with Great Britain in order that their vessels might engage in the British colonial trade. Throughout these arrangements, trade from one part of the Empire with another was kept an exclusive preserve for British ships, and by such means Huskisson believed that 'the foundation of our navigation laws will be preserved, whilst the colonies will enjoy a free trade with foreign countries, without breaking in upon the great principle of those laws in respect to foreign trade—that the cargo must be the produce of the country to which the ship belongs'.[2]

The additional details of Huskisson's scheme may be briefly summarized: (i) The old principle that non-European goods for consumption in Britain might not come from European ports even in British ships was maintained to encourage British ships to take the long haul from foreign countries in Asia, Africa, and America. It was still presumed that the long haul had a special virtue in the development of shipping.[3] (ii) The duties on goods entering the colonies were regulated by Possessions Acts, passed by the British Parliament; but, in keeping with the statute of 1778,[4] the revenue was used by the colonies. On all goods entering colonial ports, prohibitions were removed.

1 For details see 6 Geo. IV, c. 109; 6 Geo. IV, c. 114.

2 *Speeches*, ii. 317.

3 For some exceptions see 6 Geo. IV, c. 109, section 3.

4 18 Geo. III, c. 12.

The lists of duties in Possessions Acts gave a marked preference to British goods. (iii) The warehouse system with its associated fiscal privileges was extended to certain ports of the British colonies in the western hemisphere, with the purpose of making them entrepôts in the trade between Europe and the states of South America. Imported articles might be housed temporarily free of duty in bonded warehouses until they were either sold in the colony or re-exported. (iv) The large fees formerly levied in colonial ports for the benefit of public officers who had attended to the enforcement of the navigation laws were abolished. (v) Two alterations in the existing system related particularly to Mauritius and Canada. The sugar of Mauritius which formerly paid a duty of 10*s*. per cwt. more than that from the British West Indian plantations was now to be admitted at the same rate.[1] With respect to Canada, Huskisson determined 'to admit at all times, the corn of that country into our consumption, upon payment of a fixed and moderate duty. When it is considered that corn is the staple of that colony, I cannot conceive a greater act of injustice than to have declared to a part of our own Empire, as much entitled to protection as any other part of it, that against that staple the markets of this country were closed.'[2]

It may be noted that for some time Upper and Lower Canada had agitated for the admission of their corn. In 1821 the House of Assembly of Upper Canada petitioned the King against the existing law. They pointed out that the clause excluding colonial wheat from the United Kingdom when the price there was below 67*s*. per quarter had operated in the previous year for the first time to shut out Canadian wheat, with the result that cargoes of wheat and flour shipped from Quebec, when the price permitted importation, had been debarred on arrival in England and much loss was sustained. They asked that colonial grain be at all times admitted to the British Isles, subject only to a sliding duty.[3] As late as the 14 March 1825 the

[1] 6 Geo. IV, c. 76.

[2] *Speeches*, ii. 325–6.

[3] *Journals of the Legislative Assembly of Upper Canada*, 13 April 1821.

Legislative Council of Lower Canada petitioned the King against the existing corn laws:

'Being excluded from intercourse by sea for half the year, and considering that during the season of navigation the time lost before the opening of the ports to importation can be known in Canada, with that expended in preparation for shipments of grain afterwards, the benefit thereby intended to the colonies is rendered quite inefficacious as to its object.'[1]

It was further argued that normally the European exporter had an advantage over the colonial because the transport of grain from Europe to England was less expensive than from America to England. Such arguments were scarcely necessary to convince Huskisson of the wisdom of relaxing the corn laws in the interests of Canadian grain. He had long championed colonial preference as a link of Empire.

In his speech of March, Huskisson sketched the anticipated effects of his changes upon the two chief portions of Britain's Empire, the sugar islands and the continental provinces of North America. He hopefully believed that

'by opening to our sugar colonies a trade with other countries, we shall afford them, in the increased competition and economy of a direct trade, a better chance of supplying their wants on reasonable terms, and of finding a demand for their surplus productions. We shall accomplish . . . the establishment of a new course of trade, as well as of a more extended system of commission and agency, in those colonies. Mercantile houses will be formed in the principal ports, both to supply the wants of the colonies, and to watch, for their own speculations in the general markets of the world, the fluctuations of demand and price in those articles which the West Indies supply.'[2]

He looked forward to an increase in the value of property in the islands, and to a moral amelioration in the condition of society. His hope in improved economic and social conditions, with consequences beneficial to the parent state rested on the belief that 'whenever you give a free scope to capital, to industry, to the stirring intelligence and active spirit of adventure, which so strongly mark the

[1] Canadian Archives, P.F. 65.

[2] *Speeches*, ii. 319.

present times, you are in fact opening new roads to enterprise'.[1]

To the continental communities of North America freedom of trade was the *sine qua non* of their development, and its concession sound imperial statesmanship. In Huskisson's estimation it would assist in maintaining a harmonious connexion between the mother country and her daughter communities and would constitute the surest guarantee of imperial solidarity. He had a fervid faith in the destiny of the colonies under the system which he projected:

'With a tariff of duties, accounted for to their own treasury, and moreover far lighter than those paid by their neighbours—with a trade as free—with their shipping in possession of greater privileges—themselves in the enjoyment of the same civil rights,—they will not be easily moved to acts by which all these advantages may be placed in jeopardy or danger. Such a course is not in human nature. At any rate, let us, as the parent state, fulfil our duties with all proper kindness and liberality. This is true wisdom; affording us, on the one hand, the best chance of perpetuating a solid and useful connexion, and on the other, the best hope if (which God avert!) in the progress of human events, that connexion is ever to be dissolved, that the separation may not be embittered by acrimony and bloodshed; and the certain consolation that, however brought about, it will not have been hastened or provoked by vexatious interference or oppressive pretensions on our part.'[2]

Such was Huskisson's creed. Inter-imperial relations were vitiated by Britain's trade monopoly and could best be improved by its removal. Emphasis upon the links of Empire was a new note in a period of indifference to colonial interests. Huskisson shed the mercantile conception of colonies, for he believed that colonial possessions had a justification for other than trade purposes. As he viewed the Empire he was influenced almost as much by nationalist feelings as by economic considerations. The dictum of Cornewall Lewis that 'a nation derives no true glory from any possession which produced no assignable advantage to itself or to other communities' would not receive Hus-

[1] *Speeches*, ii. 320. [2] *Ibid.* 322.

kisson's acceptance. His interpretation of a national advantage was much broader than Lewis's: 'England cannot afford to be little. She must be what she is or nothing' are sentences that show an idealism for Empire which runs through the political thought of Huskisson like a silken thread and differentiates it from the bleaker utilitarianism of the vast majority of free trade thinkers.

Huskisson's policy outlined in March was duly embodied in a number of Acts which largely governed the navigation system for more than twenty years. In addition to the measures already mentioned were others with the same end in view: the encouragement of British shipping. Such was an Act repealing all quarantine duties.[1] These imposts had operated as a considerable burden on ships in quarantine. The quarantine laws were described by John Smith as a 'mass of absurdity and folly', and a petition on the subject went so far as to declare that the laws 'impede science, produce immorality, obstruct travelling, restrict commerce, navigation, and manufacture'.[2] The abolition of fees upon shipping in the colonies, and the repeal of the stamp duty payable upon the transfer of a whole ship or of any share in a ship from one person to another were other reforms. The duties on debentures for the payment of drawbacks were reduced. An alteration was also made in the consular establishments whereby British ships in foreign ports were freed from the burdensome duties imposed for the upkeep of such establishments. In the future, consuls were granted fixed and moderate salaries, paid out of the public purse. In the interests of free trade an attack was made upon the privileged position of the Levant Company, which had special trading privileges in the eastern Mediterranean. Its powerful position was undermined by Huskisson's measure whereby the Crown took from the company the appointment of consuls. This change was accompanied by the surrender of the company's charter with its conferred privileges.

The year that witnessed the opening of a new commer-

[1] 6 Geo. IV, c. 78.

[2] Hansard, 12. 995.

cial policy ended in gloom. In December 1825 London was gripped by one of the sharpest financial crises of the century. It was precipitated by the failure of the banking house of Sir Peter Pole and Company, agents for over forty country banks. The funds dropped, and as the depression continued seventy banks stopped payment. A panic seized the community, and a run on the Bank of England commenced. The vigorous action of London merchants and traders, resolved upon supporting public credit, saved England from the emergency measure of a second restriction of cash payments and from intense commercial depression. But the situation was grave. 'The state of the city', remarked Greville, 'and the terror of all bankers and merchants, as well as of all owners of property is not to be conceived but by those who witnessed it.'[1] Speculations as to the cause of the event were rife. It was generally attributed to the excessive purchasing by British merchants of goods from which a return was not immediately obtainable, and speculation in joint stock enterprises from which no economic return was ever possible. Both phenomena were assisted by the existing low rate of interest and the expansion of banking accommodations. The mania for speculation was ably described by a contemporary, Harriet Martineau:

'The acknowledgment of the independence of some of the South American states at this time turned the stream of speculation in that direction. Companies were formed to obtain . . . silver from mountain tops and clefts, where there were no workmen or tools to do the work, no fuel for the fires, and no roads or carriages to bring away the produce. There were to be pearls from the coast of Columbia; and such precious articles were to come from the other hemisphere, that sober persons began to fear too great a change in the affairs and the mind of the English people.'[2]

The collapse of the speculative bubble brought to earth those dreams and shattered the movement for reform. Huskisson's opponents groundlessly declared that the com-

[1] *Memoirs*, 65 (ed. Reeve, New York, 1875).

[2] Martineau, Harriet. *The History of England During the Peace*, i. 356 (London, 1849).

mercial depression was due directly to interference with the old fiscal navigation and commercial regulations. Hence in the succeeding year he was necessarily placed on the defensive. Further innovation in trade policy was rendered difficult in view of the sensitiveness of public opinion. Other facts also hampered reform. The year 1827 was one of the party crises: the retirement of Lord Liverpool, the brief premiership of Canning, and the rickety ministry of Goderich, which while it lasted was battered by a storm of criticism from without and dissension from within. The expulsion of Huskisson from Wellington's Cabinet was the final fact that shelved commercial and fiscal changes. The great work of reconstructive statesmanship in the twenties had closed, and fifteen years elapsed before it was adequately resumed. The colonial aspects, however, of that work require a careful survey in the next chapter.

VI

COLONIAL POLICY

THE vital and permanent achievements of Huskisson pertained to the Empire. He takes his place as an imperial statesman, imperial to a degree that Peel and Gladstone were not, for neither of them carried measures that so profoundly and directly affected the colonial possessions, and neither had such a dominant vision of a united Empire. The reforms of Wallace and Robinson with those of Huskisson transformed the colonial system upheld by British statesmen since the seventeenth century. In the eyes of the mercantilists the colonies were no more than the economic supplements of the mother-state. Their chief exports were carried in British ships, confined to channels that led to British ports, and their imports were brought from Britain, thus contributing to the revenue of the metropolis and providing her with the foremost advantage in the trade of her possessions. Thanks to the reforms of Huskisson the oversea communities were left to shape their own economic development. They were allowed to enter the field of international instead merely of imperial trade. They were substantially free in their marketing and purchasing. Their produce might be brought in either foreign or British vessels to European ports without entering Britain's narrow seas. Along with the former trade arteries leading directly to the heart of the Empire, new arteries external to the imperial body were developed.

The quotations in the preceding chapter from Huskisson's speeches illustrate the motives of his policy. These motives were two. There was, first, the idea of conceding to the colonists the economic liberty which they demanded, and in the concession to bind them to the support and maintenance of the Empire. The conviction fastened on Huskisson's mind that the concession of free trade would alone save Britain's second Empire from the fate which had befallen her first. The reform of the navigation laws was simply a robust form of constructive imperialism intended to cement the colonial possessions and comparable to the later concession of responsible government. In place of monopoly, Huskisson established imperial preference. In doing so he was influenced by the economist to whose doctrines he zealously and consistently subscribed, Adam Smith. Smith's teaching is reflected in practically every reform in the twenties, and on the subject of colonial policy the student has merely to read Huskisson's speeches to discover the economist's influence on the statesman. But there were other influences on Huskisson in addition to abstract thought. As has been pointed out in a previous chapter, there was discontent in the colonies with the commercial restrictions, and Huskisson's imperial sense prevented him from ignoring colonial sentiments. An astute politician of Upper Canada, John Beverley Robinson, wished to censure Huskisson and his colleagues by remarking that they were too much influenced by popular opinion in the colonies.[1] Huskisson would have accepted the censure as a compliment. He believed that only by considering colonial opinions and wishes could the Empire be preserved.

The changes in the navigation regulations were also to promote the interests of British manufacturers and merchants by opening foreign markets for British goods. Like the other measures of the period they were to be an instrument in breaking down protection in European states, in destroying their commercial exclusiveness, and in freeing the channels of exchange. British factories were turning out goods that must find markets, and for markets, amity with other states won by commercial concessions was essential. This is what Huskisson meant when he said that a policy which served the interests of other states would best insure those of Britain. Foreign purchasers for British products could only be obtained by allowing the colonies to become markets for foreign goods, particularly when colonial trade was opened on the basis of reciprocity.

[1] Beverley Robinson to Wilmot Horton, 25 December 1825. Q. 184 pt. 4, p. 790 (Canadian Archives).

Commercial freedom proved the prelude to self-government, although it was not meant to bear a political significance. Huskisson's vision was contained in the remark that he looked forward to 'a set of provinces emancipated from commercial thraldom, but firmly maintaining their political connexion'. He did not make clear how the political connexion was to be maintained, and he was not thinking of its maintenance through any form of colonial autonomy other than that recognized in his day. Completer colonial autonomy would have meant to him, as to his contemporaries, imperial disruption. The freedom granted was restricted to the economic life of the colonies, and even here were limitations. This fact is well illustrated by the tariffs which replaced the prohibitions of the former system. They remained under imperial control. In Wallace's Acts of 1822 arrangements were outlined for the collection of duties on articles imported to the colonies, and one statute made it clear that these duties 'shall be under the management of the commissioners of the customs in England, and shall be raised, levied, collected, paid, and recovered in such and like manner. . . as any other duties now payable to His Majesty'.[1] Similar provisions were found in Huskisson's Acts of 1825. One of the most important of these contained, (*a*) a table of prohibitions and restrictions on enumerated articles whose importation into the colonies was forbidden or restricted: (*b*) a table of duties on foreign goods entering the colonies.[2] The Imperial Parliament, which had formerly imposed the prohibitions on colonial trade and made England its entrepôt, was in the future to frame the tariffs controlling the commercial relations of the colonies with foreign states, and to this degree could exercise a great influence over colonial economic life. Huskisson and his fellow reformers did not wish to resign to colonial statesmen direction of fiscal policy. However much of the old system was sacrificed, the sovereignty of the Government in London was carefully preserved and jealously guarded. The reason is obvious. Fiscal unity was a means of developing the eco-

[1] 3 Geo. IV, c. 44.

[2] 6 Geo. IV, c. 114.

nomic resources of the whole Empire, and it could be maintained only through one authority determining policy. For this reason Huskisson, and later Durham and the colonial reformers of the thirties, left the control of duties to the authorities at Westminster.

Huskisson used this control to develop the basic feature of his system, imperial preference. Imperial preference was not new in the twenties. It had been an essential part of the old colonial system. The articles enumerated in the navigation laws were given practically a monopoly of the British market. Such was notably the case with tobacco. Its cultivation in England was even forbidden and the competition of foreigners was wholly excluded, in order to make the monopoly of the colonial product more secure. Such preference was clearly more thorough than any obtained through discriminatory duties. Preference in import duties developed in the latter part of the eighteenth century. As early as 1766 it was recognized in the corn laws. For a limited time the import of corn and grain from the colonies was allowed free of duty.[1] We have already seen how Huskisson in the corn debates of 1815 championed colonial preference and introduced it in the law of that year. In the succeeding years he remained its consistent defender. With no less vigour he upheld fiscal preference on colonial timber. From early times the colonies were looked upon as sources of timber supply, and many measures bore witness to the endeavour of the imperial authorities to encourage the colonies in developing these resources. In Anne's reign a bounty was granted on imports of British American masts, yards, and bowsprits,[2] and in the reign of George I all timber imported from the colonies in British vessels was freed from duty.[3] But throughout the eighteenth century the timber preference was of little significance, because the duties on the foreign product were low, and the freight charges on colonial imports placed the foreigner and the colonist on much the same footing. Not until the Napoleonic period did the preference become of

[1] 6 Geo. III, c. 3.

[2] 3 and 4 Anne, c. 10.

[3] 8 Geo. I, c. 1, sec. 2.

first importance, and notwithstanding the changes of 1821 remained so until the administration of Peel.

With Huskisson's defence of colonial preference it was a case of the imperialist overriding the economist. He was forced to defend the system against the assaults of those with whom his ideas on free trade were otherwise in agreement. Economists like Ricardo and M'Culloch had scant sympathy with a preference, particularly if it interfered with buying in the cheapest market. In their opinion it was bad economics. Ricardo attacked the preference on Canadian timber. He stated that by purchasing timber from Canada instead of from the north of Europe the country lost £400,000 a year, while of the preference for West Indian sugar he declared that 'the people of England paid grievously for their sugar, without a corresponding benefit to any persons. The sum which they paid was swallowed up in the fruitless waste of human labour.' [1] The farmers no less strongly opposed a policy which might turn the colonists into their competitors, while the shipping interests in the Baltic trade disliked a preference on colonial timber since it injured their shipping. These various interests had their representatives in Parliament, and in 1825 strong pressure was brought on Huskisson to reduce the preference on Canadian timber, but he was emphatic in answer that it had a vital justification.[2] It maintained a large British shipping, and it developed an important industry in the North American colonies.

Imperial preference as nurtured and promoted by Huskisson had three important aspects: (i) There was fiscal discrimination in favour of colonial as against foreign products in the mother country, notably in the corn, sugar, and timber duties. Such discrimination bulked in importance when Britain departed from prohibitions and high protection. Short of wholly excluding foreign products it was only through fiscal discrimination that she could confer benefits on her colonies. (ii) There was discrimination in favour of British as against foreign products in the colonies.

[1] See his speeches on, 5 April 1821, Hansard, 2nd ser., 5; 17 May 1822, Hansard, 2nd ser., 7.

[2] *Speeches* ii, 362.

The products of Britain or of other colonies entered a colonial port on a preferential basis. This form of preference is readily distinguished from that conceded in the twentieth century to British goods by the dominions in that the amount of the duties was fixed by the imperial and not by the colonial authorities. (iii) Inter-imperial trade was confined to British and colonial ships. This provision was more a prohibition than a preference, since it shut out foreign vessels altogether from the trade routes within the Empire. Although it was the maintenance of a strongly protectionist clause in the old navigation code, Huskisson cherished it, for in his estimation it assisted in the development of a powerful imperial marine.

Such was Huskisson's colonial system. How did it meet the needs of the Empire? This question may be examined from two angles: the effect and reception of the system in the colonies, and its effect and reception in Britain. In Britain it was received graciously and with enthusiastic welcome by those of Liberal leanings. Thinkers and politicians influenced by the teachings of Adam Smith and Ricardo—and there were few in that age not influenced by the economists—hailed the Huskisson reforms as a great advance. *The Times* and the *Edinburgh Review* pronounced his measures as wholesome and desirable in every degree. In sympathy with his reforms *The Times* passed on him a panegyric.

'We look upon Mr. Huskisson to be the most useful minister that England has had to boast of for many years. It is not merely that he has reasoned upon experimental questions with more discrimination and acuteness than his neighbours, but that he has watched the relative play of the national interests upon each other, with more patient and steady vigilance; embracing gradually and leisurely within his view, a wider field of facts by which to qualify his principles, as well as to support them.' [1]

Manufacturers and others who felt the pinch of contracted markets looked hopefully to these reforms as a means of enabling British trade to get on its feet. To some it appeared certain that a new era of trade expansion would

[1] *The Times*, 30 May 1827.

result from the relaxations in the navigation code, and this hopefulness had much to do with the excessive speculation in 1825.

But amidst the warm welcome were voices of criticism. Conservative interests, hostile to changes of any kind, viewed with dread the possible effects of Huskisson's reforms. The Tories whom *Blackwood's* represented considered that Huskisson and his colleagues had brought the Empire to the edge of disaster. To them the freedom of colonial trade simply meant that producers in Britain no longer felt sure of colonial markets, and that the shipping industry was exposed to a ruthless competition with foreigners. *Blackwood's* in one of its more moderate articles remarked:

'The new colonial system at its birth professed to open the colonial market to the manufactures and produce of all nations, at moderate and not prohibitory duties; and likewise to the ships of all nations, on condition of reciprocity. With regard to foreign manufactures and produce, this system has naturally had the most partial operation. Some kinds are as effectively excluded by its duties as they were by the old prohibition; and other kinds are admitted, to the exclusion of British manufactures and produce. It thus operates in the most unjust manner to the community at home. From some parts it takes away their colonial trade, and to other parts it does no injury.'[1]

The shipping interest in particular considered itself injured by Huskisson's reforms, and amongst its representatives there was consternation. It looked upon the navigation laws as its bulwark, and the monopoly of the carrying trade to and from the colonies as the chief cause of its growth. For two centuries navigation laws and colonies were viewed as the most important means of developing shipping, just as shipping was the one source of an invincible navy. Hence, when the monopoly of the colonial trade was taken away, the British shipowners naturally felt that the essential foundations of their industry had disappeared. Decay and disaster must irretrievably come. In 1825 and in the succeeding years deputations of shipowners frequently laid their case before Huskisson, and their general

[1] *Blackwood's*, September, 1828.

grievance was their alleged inability to compete with foreigners, because the latter paid lower wages, lived in untaxed countries, and built their ships at less cost. In June 1826 a deputation of the Liverpool Shipowners Association maintained that the cost of an English built ship was double that of a ship constructed in the ports of northern Europe, and the expenses of navigation amounted to three times the cost of sailing a foreign vessel.[1]

They hastened with their case to Parliament. Their mouthpiece was General Gascoyne, who in the spring of 1827 painted lurid pictures of the decay and suffering that had befallen the shipping interest. England's chief source of wealth and power was according to this gallant champion profoundly undermined. The palladium of the Empire was endangered. Gascoyne's attack combined with the many petitions from the shipowners prophesying disaster led Huskisson on 7 May 1827 to deliver an able defence of his commercial and colonial policy.[2] He flatly denied any truth in the statements that the British shipping industry had suffered from the new policy, and showed how the claims of the petitioners were completely unsubstantiated. Indeed they were incapable of being substantiated. In 1826 the amount of British tonnage entered inwards was larger than in any previous year with the exception of 1825. It is needless to reproduce Huskisson's statistics. His defence, however, was complete and decisive, and he caught the ear and confidence of the House by his claim that 'all the measures in question were called for by the circumstances of the times in which we live, and by a due regard to the true interests of the country'. So triumphant was his case that the shipowners failed to get a committee to investigate their grievances. Though defeated in Parliament they continued throughout the country their campaign against the new system. Pamphlets appeared denouncing Huskisson's opinions and prophesying ruin to the Empire from their effects.[3] He was described

[1] *The Times*, 21 June 1826. [2] *Speeches*, iii. 77.

[3] e.g. *Two Letters in Reply to the Speech of the Rt. Hon. W. Huskisson*, by Mercator (London, 1827). *A Letter to the Rt. Hon. W. Huskisson on the*

as an adventurer and theorist who to satisfy his interest in the abstract ideas of political economy played with the destiny of Great Britain. His defence of the new policy was repudiated as sophistry, and his figures with respect to the tonnage of British shipping were discarded as misleading.[1] Freed from violent statements the claims of the shipowners were concisely expressed by one of their pamphleteers:

'That they have been forced, without sufficient cause and without any protection, into a competition with the shipping of the north of Europe, which it is not possible for them to carry on without ruin to themselves; and further, that the ultimate consequences of such competition must be the entire destruction of the carrying trade in British bottoms to those countries with which treaties of reciprocity have been made.'[2]

Such substantially remained their arguments. They dreaded competition with the Scandinavian countries because these countries were supposed to build ships more cheaply and to pay less wages to their crews. Their wail of distress continued after Huskisson's death. In the thirties the shipping interests were amongst the most discontented, and they were disturbed by the same fears. In 1833 a report of the Shipowners Society set forth that

'the long continued and still existing depression of the shipping interest, the partial production and great aggravation of distress, caused by continual changes in our navigation system, the utter impossibility of the successful maintenance of an unrestricted competition with foreign navigation, the gross injustice of the imposition of peculiar and exclusive burdens on maritime commerce for purposes purely national, while exposed to that competition; the declining quality and estimation of British tonnage; the embarrassment, decay and ruin of the British shipowners may now be viewed as incontrovertible propositions.'[3]

Was this claim of absolute ruin valid? If the statistics

Effects of Free Trade in our Shipping Colonies and Commerce, by S. Atkinson (London, 1827).

[1] See *Glasgow Courier*, 31 May 1827.

[2] Mercator, *Two Letters in Reply to the Speech of the Rt. Hon. W. Huskisson*, p. 2. (London, 1827).

[3] Quoted in Ricardo, J. L., *The Anatomy of the Navigation Laws*, 43 (London, 1847).

of British tonnage can be taken as evidence of the strength of shipping, the claim was groundless. Of course the case was argued pro and con with elaborate references to statistics; but those which best stand verification are decidedly against the shipowners, and prove that instead of the Huskisson system inflicting injury on British shipping it conferred benefits. Without going into the details, the evidence of a reliable authority may be given. In 1847 a select committee of the Commons sat on the navigation laws and examined some thirty witnesses. The most illuminating evidence was that of G. R. Porter, director of the statistical department of the Board of Trade. He showed clearly that British shipping did not suffer from Huskisson's reforms.[1] In 1824 the total tonnage from British possessions under the navigation laws entering British ports amounted to 893,097 tons. In 1846 it was 1,735,924 tons, or an increase of 94·37 per cent. This tonnage was of course protected from foreigners, but the percentage increase of unprotected tonnage was even greater. In 1824 British tonnage inwards from foreign countries amounted to 904,223 tons. In 1846 after twenty-two years of competition with foreigners it was 2,558,809 tons, being an increase of 183 per cent. Such figures are sufficiently convincing, and are supported by many pages of other statistical evidence. British shipping did not decline in the period after Huskisson's Acts. It increased. Even in the trade with Britain's powerful rival, the United States, British shipping grew in magnitude: 'In 1821 the proportion of British vessels which entered the ports of the United States was $7\frac{1}{5}$ per cent., compared with the American tonnage employed in the foreign trade of the States; while in 1835, that proportion was increased to 39 per cent., which proportion was maintained in 1844, and increased in 1849 to $55\frac{3}{4}$ per cent.'[2] It cannot be claimed that the increase was due directly and solely to Huskisson's measures, but it was due to the general

[1] See his evidence quoted in Ricardo, J. L., *The Anatomy of the Navigation Laws*, p. 40 (London, 1847). Ricardo was on the committee.

[2] Porter, *Progress of the Nation*, 391–2 (London, 1851).

increase of trade which in large part resulted from the relaxations in the old commercial system.

The reception and effects in the colonies of Huskisson's Acts remain to be discussed. While the attitude of the colonists varied according to their particular interests, in general they at first received the reforms as a great charter of economic liberty. When news of them reached Halifax the public buildings were illuminated and a civic demonstration of satisfaction was staged. In other colonies the reception of the tidings was of a similar nature. An able and enlightened Nova Scotian editor undertook to state what would be the effects of the new system:

'We are a commercial as much as an agricultural people, and must derive our full proportion of the benefit which will occur to all the colonies as above stated from a freedom of trade. It is now in our power to buy at the cheapest and sell at the dearest rate. Wherever our commodities will command the highest price or the articles we want can be purchased on the lowest terms, thither we can repair. In buying manufactured goods, we are no longer restricted to the British market, but may import canvas from Russia, iron from Sweden, linens from Germany, silks and broadcloths from France, and from the Mediterranean and the United States all the infinite variety of their manufactures and productions. This is surely an advantage of immense value, as it will furnish new materials of trade, and add to our comforts and enjoyments a thousand articles of consumption. But we cannot expect to undergo so prodigious a change without experiencing some loss. Every great revolution in affairs brings distress and ruin on many individuals and many branches of employment. . . . It is undeniable that certain trades in this province and especially in Halifax, will be injured, perhaps destroyed by a new and powerful competition. The manufacturers of tobacco complain that the duty of 20 per cent. will not afford them adequate protection, and that even with that advantage their rivals in the southern states will undersell them. So the tanners, leather cutters, tallow chandlers, chocolate makers, shoemakers, and other trades are afraid of the competition, and predict the ruin, or at least the diminished profits of their several occupations. We shall not attempt to console these individuals by false hopes; for though we think their fears much exaggerated we agree that many of them will be injured, and sympathize in their misfortune.'[1]

[1] *Nova Scotian* (Halifax), 4 May 1825.

This forecast of the likely effects of Huskisson's policy was well borne out by the events of subsequent years. There was general satisfaction with the commercial freedom, but many manufacturers grumbled at the duties levied by the Imperial Government, while in the West Indies it was claimed that the duties were so high as greatly to raise the cost of living to the planters.[1] In Nova Scotia, the oldest of the continental colonies, some manufacturers clamoured for higher protection against the Americans, and asked that the raw products brought from the United States and used in manufacture, such as hides, tallow, pitch, and turpentine be admitted free.[2]

Very different was the demand from Upper Canada that in some cases the duties on imported goods were too high. One newspaper called the Colonial Trade Acts the scourge of the colony, and hoped 'that measures will be adopted to protect us against the ruinous effects of laws passed by persons wholly ignorant of our local situation and peculiar wants'.[3] The writer instanced the 30 per cent. duty on printing paper as excessive, since all the paper used in the colony was imported from the United States. A colony like Upper Canada with few manufactures would naturally suffer from tariffs framed by imperial authorities. Hence in the eyes of many colonists the one serious defect in Huskisson's colonial system was the determination of fiscal policy in London. The colonial assemblies might impose duties for revenue, but the giving or withholding of protection rested with the Parliament at Westminster, and it was seldom well acquainted with the effect of its tariffs upon colonial interests. McGregor in his evidence before the select committee on import duties in 1840 mentioned the discontent in the colonies with the prohibitions and imperial duties. J. D. Hume before the same committee

1 For criticisms of Huskisson's tariff in its effects upon the West Indies see Alexander Macdonnell, *Colonial Commerce*, 112–21 (London, 1828), and Sir Henry Parnell, *Financial Reform*, ch. xv (London, 1831).

2 *Nova Scotian*, 25 May 1825.

3 Quoted from the *Canadian Freeman* in the *Nova Scotian*, 4 January 1826.

argued that the imperial duties ought to be abolished. They were merely vexations to the colonists, and brought little revenue to the imperial exchequer. He stated that in the year 1832 the produce of the imperial duties in the West Indies was £75,340, and the payment of custom houses amounted to £68,028, leaving only £7,312 for the revenue.[1]

Another colonial complaint concerned a provision in the new navigation law which Huskisson greatly emphasized; viz., that inter-imperial trade remained the monopoly of British shipowners. Goods exported from Canada to the British Isles or to another colony must be carried in British ships. Canadian merchants and West Indian planters grumbled that this remnant of the old navigation law frequently inconvenienced them. Often when they wished to send goods to other parts of the Empire there was a scarcity of British freighters in their ports, and because they were prohibited from using American or other foreign vessels goods remained for long in their warehouses. Hence American merchants had a considerable advantage over them, because they could use either American or British ships, and freights were likely to be lowest to the merchant with the widest choice of ships. Moreover, the clause gave rise to other inconveniences. Samuel Browning, a whale-merchant and shipowner of New South Wales, gave an example in his evidence, in 1847, before the committee on the operation and policy of the navigation laws.[2] At Swan River, in Australia, in 1842 and 1843, there was a scarcity of rice. An American vessel discharged an assorted cargo of produce, sailed, and returned in a few weeks with a cargo of rice. On its return the custom authorities would not allow the captain to land his produce, because he brought it from another British colony. The rice was worth 3½*d.* or 4*d.* a pound at Swan River, but the American was forced to sell it to a captain of an English vessel belonging to Sydney who carried it back to that port where

[1] *Report*, pp. 76, 121–3.

[2] See *Five Reports of Commons Committee on the Operation and Policy of the Navigation Laws* (1847), p. 117.

it would be sold at not more than ½*d*. a pound, notwithstanding that the colony of Swan River was in the greatest need of rice. Canadian and West Indian merchants frequently complained of similar inconveniences.

In examining the dissatisfaction with the colonial system of Huskisson we get back to the fundamental fact that the fiscal and trade regulations were still framed by the Imperial Government. General criticism in the colonies of this control was frequent between 1825 and 1848. In 1835 a select committee of the legislative assembly of Upper Canada lamented that

'laws for the regulation of our trade and commerce are enacted in the parliament of the United Kingdom, and continually changed and varied without our being consulted for our interest, although the value of our labour and property is unduly affected by this ever-varying system of legislation.' [1]

In 1839 a member of the Upper Canadian Assembly, Hamilton Merritt, wrote interesting letters to the Lieutenant-Governor, Sir George Arthur.[2] He remarked that it was impossible for the Imperial Government successfully to regulate the duties on articles entering the Canadian provinces, because the Imperial Parliament misunderstood Canadian conditions. He referred to the existing tariff as evidence of how poorly British control served Canadian interests. It actually discouraged the use of the St. Lawrence waterway for inland trade as compared with its American rivals. He believed that if no restrictions were placed on the passage of American products down the St. Lawrence, that waterway would attract the trade of the entire north-west, and Montreal would rival New York as a port of export. His suggestions are sufficiently interesting to bear quotation:

'By placing the duties wholly under the control of [the colonial] legislature, they will of course be regulated and disposed of in accordance with the motives and principles by which mankind are in general governed. Their interest will be first to increase the revenue of the province, by closely watching any change in the duties on any

1 *Journals of Legislative Assembly*, 1835, app. i, no. 2, p. 2.
2 Upper Canada Sundries, February 1839 (Canadian Archives).

given article at the port of New York. By lessening the duty on that article at the port of Quebec and increasing it at the interior ports from the United States, we secure its introduction at a Canadian seaport and through Canadian waters, an effect which besides securing the revenue now lost gives the best evidence that it will promote the interests of the British and Canadian merchant, who will under this additional protection introduce the whole of his stock at the port of Quebec. The beneficial result of this change would be inevitable. We could so regulate the duty on each article consumed that a large revenue could be at once acquired. This would pay the interest upon the cost of constructing the St. Lawrence canal until completed. The moment that work was completed, the tolls derived from American commerce alone would pay the cost of construction, and those duties could be entirely abolished.' [1]

Criticism of imperial control was not confined to Hamilton Merritt. In 1840 the House of Assembly of the Canadas submitted an address to the Governor, Poulett Thomson, asking that the legislature be empowered to alter the trade regulations of the colony in cases wherever the special interests of the colony might be promoted. Thomson transmitted the address to the Imperial Government, with interesting remarks of his own. While admitting that the Imperial Government should regulate the general principles of colonial trade, he confessed that he was

'obliged to observe the great inconveniences, and even loss, which results to the colony from the necessity which now exists for all changes in this respect originating in England. There are a vast number of small points seriously affecting the interests of colonial trade and not at all disturbing the general principle or objects sought to be established by imperial legislation, in which a change is frequently found to be desirable. Great difficulty exists in the first place in explaining the points at home and next in proving that they are of sufficient importance to demand legislation there, but even if this be done I know myself from experience in that department, how much difficulty and delay unavoidably arise in carrying such measures through parliament.' [2]

[1] Hamilton Merritt to Sir George Arthur, 13 February 1839. Upper Canada Sundries (Canadian Archives).

[2] Thomson to Lord John Russell, 26 May 1840, Series Q. 272, pt. i. 195–6 (Canadian Archives).

He recommended that the colonial legislature be empowered to originate measures of this description. His dispatch is of particular interest in view of the fact that he was a disciple and a successor of Huskisson as President of the Board of Trade, where he ably defended and maintained the Huskisson system.

It is needless to discuss further the dissatisfaction in the colonies with Huskisson's system. It would undoubtedly have been more pronounced amongst the mercantile classes but for the existence of the colonial preference in the British market. Preference was the preservative element in the system built by Huskisson. It was a valuable compensation for other disadvantages. So significant did it appear to some British public men that they considered it to be the sole bond of Empire. Sir Robert Peel did so. In 1842 he stated in the House of Commons,

> 'You shall treat your colonies without discrimination, as foreign countries. . . . If that principle be correct, there is an end of your colonial system. If you sanction this proposition, then you ought also to say, "let the colonies assert their own independence, and provide for their own maintenance".' [1]

Yet the preferences consistently championed by Huskisson and Peel did not escape criticism in the colonies. There was initial ground for dissatisfaction in that the principal preferences, those on timber and grain, did not apply to the products of the Australian states. They applied only to the products of the British North American colonies which considered them inadequate. Huskisson was largely instrumental in getting a preference for the grain of the northern provinces, yet the colonists were never wholly satisfied with the amount of that preference. Reference has already been made to the address of the Assembly of the Canadas in 1840, where it is stated:

> 'Your Majesty's faithful Commons are aware that the products of these colonies are admitted into the ports of the mother country at a duty of 5*s*. per quarter, when wheat is below an average of 67*s*. per quarter; but from the expenses of transportation from the

[1] Hansard, 3rd ser., 63. 546.

interior to the sea, and thence to the United Kingdom, experience proves they derive very little advantage from this protection.'[1]

They asked that the duty of *5s.* per quarter be taken off. In full justice to Huskisson it may be said that he would have been willing to admit colonial grain free, but the British agriculturists would not tolerate it and fought vigorously against Peel's later more generous concessions. The fact is that Huskisson obtained for the colonies the best fiscal considerations possible under the circumstances, and if the colonists grumbled they could cast little blame on him.

Peel has been mentioned as a defender of preference. His tariff of 1842 embodied it in the duties on 375 articles out of 825.[2] Yet it was he who within four years swept away imperial preference and brought the Huskisson system toppling down. It is not necessary to tell the story of Peel's budgets, culminating in that of 1846 which practically destroyed the preferential tariff. Immediately there was a storm of criticism in the colonies. Those portions of the Huskisson arrangements to which exception had long been taken were bluntly denounced; i. e. the remaining navigation regulations and the imperial control over colonial duties. In Montreal a free trade association of prominent merchants was formed to agitate for the complete economic liberty of the colony,[3] and some were led aside to worship the alien god of American annexation. In other colonies similar opinions were expressed, and the Government responded by quick action on the subject of duties. In 1846 the Russell ministry passed a statute empowering the Queen to assent to Acts of the colonial legislatures to abolish the differential duties in favour of British goods.[4] In other words, to the colonies was left the task of sweeping away fiscal preferences. What the Imperial Parliament under the influence of Huskisson and his col-

[1] Series Q. 272, pt. i (Canadian Archives).

[2] 5 and 6 Vict. c. 47.

[3] See the pamphlet issued by the Association, *Address of the Free Trade Association to the Inhabitants of Canada*, March 1846.

[4] 9 and 10 Vict. c. 91.

leagues had established, the colonial legislatures were to abolish.

It is an old truth that the removal of one popular grievance gives room for another. Dissatisfaction with the existing navigation regulations now became pronounced, particularly in the Canadas where it was felt that they prevented the adequate use of the St. Lawrence waterway and raised the cost of shipping. The evidence taken in 1847 before the committee on the navigation laws showed the state of colonial opinion. But in the spring of 1848 in order to inform the Imperial Government of all the facts, the executive council of the Canadian provinces sent a long memorial across the Atlantic.[1] They stated that so long as colonial products had a preference in the markets of Britain, the monopoly of the carrying trade by British ships was tolerable, but now this monopoly was a sore grievance. They advanced the old argument that, if American and foreign vessels were allowed to carry Canadian produce to Britain, Canadian merchants would reap the benefits of cheap freights. Enthusiastically they saw as a consequence of this liberty the great St. Lawrence waterway become the chief channel of trade for the American continent. In the following year the British Government bowed to colonial opinion and the pressure of merchants at home. It repealed the Navigation Act.

Thus perished the colonial system of Huskisson. Preferential duties for the promotion of inter-imperial commerce and navigation regulations for the maintenance of an imperial mercantile marine were swept aside with the triumph of free trade. In their nature Huskisson's arrangements had been transitional. They could not endure, for they were an unsatisfactory half-way house between the old status of monopoly and complete colonial liberty in economic matters. Even without Peel's crucial legislation in 1846 the colonies in time would have demanded complete fiscal liberty and freedom from navigation restraints. Such a demand was an inevitable result of self-governing

[1] Elgin to Grey, 12 May 1848. Series G. v. 461, 208 (Canadian Archives).

aspirations. Huskisson's vision of a self-sufficing Empire nurtured through fiscal preferences was statesmanlike, but it could be realized, if at all, only through the assent of the colonies recognized in the construction of their own tariffs. The British Empire has long awaited the attainment on such a basis of Huskisson's preferential scheme.

Huskisson's place in British history rests upon the system just described. But his name was linked with some minor questions of Empire concerning which discussion is necessary. What appeared to contemporaries as one of the most acute problems in the twenties was that of negro slavery in the most cherished portion of the Empire, the West Indies. No problem gave rise to such heated controversy, not even the navigation laws and Huskisson's commercial policy. The gladiators of contemporary journalism found in this question a cause for uncompromising conflict, and erected it into the one vital issue of the Empire. One party in Britain, dubbed the anti-colonians, attacked slavery, and their demands extended from a regulation of the system to its complete abolition. This group included leaders who from their agitation have obtained a place in British history, Buxton, Clarkson, Zachariah Macaulay, James Stephen, and Wilberforce who never took his eyes from the promised land of negro freedom. However lofty might be their aims, they were often fiercely immoderate in the statement of their case and bitter towards those who in the colonies had vested interests in the preservation of slavery. Before half of the decade had passed, leaders like Macaulay had moments when, losing hope of inducing the colonial legislatures to effect even mitigatory legislation, they demanded the direct interference of the Imperial Government. Some were so exasperated by the attitude of the planters that they were in favour of severing connexion with the recalcitrant colonies. They declared that the British merchants should turn their trade from the West Indies to the East Indies and China, and that the planters be left to stew in their own juice.

The slave-owners had champions in Britain, but the

anti-colonians had a decided advantage. They were pleading a moral cause, and being far from the West Indies they could introduce an element of exaggeration into the descriptions of conditions there. But one fact protected the planters. Practically all of the West India islands had legislatures, and measures which the British Parliament might introduce to regulate or to remove slavery would seriously cut across powers conceded to these legislative bodies. Thus the question of slavery broadened into a constitutional issue, and the interference of the Imperial Parliament bristled with difficulties. In May 1823 an important debate on the subject occurred. On 15 May Fowell Buxton moved a resolution:

'that the state of slavery is repugnant to the principles of the British constitution and of the Christian religion, and that it ought to be abolished gradually throughout the British colonies, with as much expedition as may be found consistent with a due regard to the well-being of the parties concerned.' [1]

Buxton hoped that there might be immediate enactments which would obtain the freedom of all children born after a certain day, and would mitigate the condition of such slaves as could never be freed. Canning representing Huskisson and his group approved the end sought by Buxton, but considered it unwise to fix an assignable date for the abolition of slavery.

Much to the alarm of the West Indian interests, Buxton's resolutions were carried. West Indian property immediately fell in the market, and when a report of the debate reached the planters their resentment was defiant. In Jamaica the House of Assembly talked passionately of independence should the Imperial Parliament attempt to dictate to them. In other colonies the resolutions were received with like hostility, and the missionaries who championed abolition were ill treated. In Demerara the negroes, thinking that the King of England had freed them, rose against their masters, and the island was placed under martial law for five months. In 1824 the Imperial

[1] Hansard, 2nd ser., 9. 257.

Government followed up its resolutions of the previous year by an order in council embodying such measures as seemed most necessary for ameliorating the condition of the negroes. This order was sent both to the colonies where the Crown had the power to command and to those with local legislatures. To the latter it was accompanied by strong representations that its principles be adopted. It appears from the debates in 1826 that the leading colonies did little to carry out the suggestions of the Government, and this fact stirred the abolitionists to violent suggestions. But the Government was convinced that more could be done by winning the co-operation of the colonial legislatures than by antagonizing them, and such was the opinion of Huskisson. He looked forward to the eventual emancipation of the negro population, but considered that it could not with expediency be hurried. He believed that British influence should be exercised upon the slave colonies for the amelioration of slavery and for the gradual transition from slavery to freedom. In November 1823 he wrote to Sir John Gladstone, father of William Ewart Gladstone that:

'it is only by gradual amelioration . . . by moral and religious improvement . . . by humanity and kindness, by imperceptibly creating better domestic habits and feelings among the slaves, by countenancing and encouraging all that can have that tendency in the conduct of the owners and white people . . . by repressing with the strong arm of law, and stigmatizing with the moral powers of opprobrium and disgrace whatever leads to an opposite result, that we can have a chance of ultimately and even then remotely, providing for the termination of so great an evil.' [1]

In the same letter he criticized Wilberforce and his associates whose agitation he blamed for the negro rebellion at Demerara. In April 1824 the letter was surreptiously published in *The Times*, and earned for Huskisson the resentment of the abolitionists.[2]

During his brief tenure in the Colonial Office, Huskisson was pushed into more intimate and vexatious contact with

[1] Huskisson to John Gladstone, 2 November 1823, B.M. Add. MS. 38, 745, f. 79 b.

[2] *The Times*, 27 April 1824.

the problem. One of his first official dispatches as minister was to the Lieutenant-Governor of Jamaica, Sir John Keane, in which he intimated that the Government was forced to disallow the statute passed by the Assembly of Jamaica for altering the slave laws. While conciliatory, and showing due consideration to the feelings of the Jamaican Assembly, Huskisson took exception to the discriminations in the Act against the religious missions of Wesleyans and Moravians, which he believed played a useful part in contributing to the religious and moral instruction of the slaves. The Jamaican Assembly had scant sympathy with the missionaries whom they viewed as the chief promoters of negro discontent. Huskisson was dissatisfied with other points in the proposed law, particularly the omission of restraints upon the corporal punishment of the slaves. But the significance of the dispatch is contained not so much in its specific criticisms as in its general emphasis upon the need of ameliorating the lot of the slave. It reflected Huskisson's ruling opinion that the colonies themselves should undertake the mitigation of slave conditions in preparation for the ultimate freedom of the negro, and that the mother country should confine itself to suggestions and exhortations. He stated in the following year that:

'if there should be no accordance of feeling between the Government of this country and the local legislatures, any attempt to carry the projected improvements into effect would only throw the colonies into irretrievable ruin without in the least degree benefiting the slave population.' [1]

As the colonists should be free to pursue their trade expansion unhampered by navigation regulations, they should no less be free to fashion policy on such a thorny issue as slavery. The mother country might exhort and suggest, but must not attempt to coerce. This policy failed to satisfy the abolitionists; but it was in line with the Liberalism which Huskisson had successfully championed in other spheres, and possibly had it been followed longer the later abolition of slavery would have come without the evil consequences that actually accompanied it.

[1] *Speeches*, iii. 238.

An imperial subject lacking the publicity of slavery, but of outstanding interest in the twenties was emigration. The depression after the Napoleonic war brought sharp distress, and well-meaning men championed emigration as a relief. In Parliament its most ardent and tireless advocate was Wilmot Horton, who from 1821 had been Under-Secretary of State for War and the Colonies and was in such close association with Huskisson that he followed the latter from Wellington's ministry. Huskisson shared much of Horton's enthusiasm for the promotion of emigration, and both earned the wrathful denunciation of *Blackwood's* for their 'speculative views' on the subject. Thanks to Horton's activity committees were appointed in 1826 and 1827 to investigate the possibilities of emigration and its general effects.[1] Both committees reported a redundancy of able-bodied labourers in Britain with the consequence that wages in many cases were reduced below the level of subsistence. They recommended emigration as a wholesome remedy, and the committee of 1827 suggested that it could be carried out on a large scale by the advance of public money to emigrants on a security for its repayment. But the results of Horton's reports were meagre. After the report of 1827 Colonel Cockburn was sent to survey lands in the colonies of Nova Scotia, New Brunswick, and Prince Edward Island, and to make preparation for 10,000 emigrants. His labour was nullified by the failure of the Government to undertake the colonization plans. In April 1828 Horton introduced a Bill to enable parishes in England, under given regulations and for a limited period, to mortgage their poor-rates for the purpose of assisting voluntary emigration, but the Bill failed to pass.

Huskisson viewed emigration both as a means of relieving congestion within the country and as a method of building a greater Britain across the seas, which would afford employment to the industry and capital of the people at home.[2] Anticipating the opinions of the colonial reformers

[1] See Hansard, 2nd ser., 18. 939 for Horton's summary of the reports.

[2] *Speeches*, iii. 471.

of the thirties, he emphasized that emigration must not be the mere shovelling out of paupers, and that those who emigrated should carry enough capital to assist them in the new world:

'It is only the connexion of property with population, that can render emigration useful to this country, or beneficial to the colonists. It is only such a principle of emigration that can strengthen the colonies, benefit the empire from which they proceeded, and open new markets to the mother country, by multiplying the consumption of her products.' [1]

He was also interested in relieving the miseries of the emigrants in their voyages across the Atlantic. The torturing conditions under which they lived for months in congested and ill-equipped ships were dolefully pictured in the State Papers of the period. Imagination can scarcely highten the miserableness of the emigrants under such conditions. Typical of many reports was a dispatch in 1827 of Sir James Kempt, Lieutenant-Governor in Nova Scotia:

'There this day arrived in the *Big James* from Waterford one hundred and twenty passengers of the most wretched description, all of whom as well as the whole crew . . . are labouring under typhus fever. One hundred and sixty embarked from Ireland, five died at sea, and the vessel being obliged to put into St. John, Newfoundland, for medical assistance and provisions, thirty-five were left behind there too ill to proceed. The disease among these miserable people was occasioned solely by their scanty nourishment during the voyage, by the crowded and filthy state of the ship, and by a want of medical assistance.' [2]

Horton in the Commons gave abundant evidence of the prevalence of these conditions and of the lamentable consequences that resulted from such emigrants being dumped in the colonies. Huskisson pointed out that emigrants crossing in this fashion 'carried with them contagious disorders of the worst description. In some instances the gaol fever devastated whole townships, to the destruction of not less than one-tenth of the population.' [3] The evil was

[1] *Ibid.* 473.

[2] Sir James Kempt to Viscount Goderich, 7 September 1827, L.O. 217 v. 197, p. 95 (Canadian Archives).

[3] *Speeches*, iii. 230.

rendered all the greater by the poverty of the emigrants and their frequent inability to procure a livelihood under the novel conditions of colonial life. Huskisson and Horton both agreed that the conditions on the emigrant ships should as far as possible be regulated by law. In 1825 an Act had been passed, but repealed two years later. In 1828 Horton, backed enthusiastically by Huskisson, re-enacted essentially the same measure.[1] Notwithstanding the ample evidence in support of such a law, it encountered considerable opposition particularly from the doctrinaire champion of *laisser-faire*. Hume characteristically attacked it on the ground that it checked the free movement of population, and twitted Huskisson on how he, a champion of free trade, could consistently support such a measure. No less characteristic was Huskisson's retort that 'he was unable to understand the nature of those pure abstract principles, which were to prevent them from interfering where the interests of humanity were at stake. He could not conceive the meaning of those general principles which should never bend to circumstances.'[2] The aim of the Bill, Huskisson pointed out, was not to restrain the colonies in obtaining emigrants but simply to insure for the emigrants wholesome conditions of travel in order to prevent the introduction of such fatal fevers as had taken a heavy toll of the population in some colonial settlements. Not merely was it humanity to the emigrants but it was also dictated by consideration of colonial interests: 'We had no fair right to inundate them with such a population as they were receiving under the existing system.'[3]

It must be confessed that notwithstanding the passage of this Act no real improvement was effected. Ten years later Durham described conditions on the emigrant ships very similar to those which Huskisson and Horton wished to remedy. He quoted Dr. Morin, inspecting physician at Quebec, as stating that he was

'at a loss for words to describe the state in which the emigrants frequently arrived; with few exceptions, the state of the ships was

[1] 9 Geo. IV, c. 21, known as the Passengers' Act.

[2] *Speeches*, iii. 231.

[3] *Ibid.* 234.

quite abominable; so much so, that the harbour-master's boatmen had no difficulty, at the distance of gun-shot, either when the wind was favourable or in a dead calm, in distinguishing by the odour alone a crowded emigrant ship.' [1]

Huskisson's Act was inadequately enforced, and in addition its provisions were probably not sufficiently comprehensive to check abuses. It illustrates the tentative character of early measures pertaining to emigration. There was no serious effort in the twenties to think out clearly the problems, and amongst doctrinaire Liberals there was a belief that sea captains should not be interfered with in whatever arrangements they made for the accommodation of emigrants. Emigration questions were not seriously considered by public men until the organization in 1830 of Gibbon Wakefield's Colonization Society with the object in Wakefield's words 'to substitute systematic colonization for mere emigration, and on a scale sufficient to produce important effects on the mother country'. It was an enterprise that even in the thirties did not receive widespread support, but one can scarcely be wrong in claiming that Huskisson would have given it his whole-hearted blessing.

We have already seen how Huskisson advanced the commercial freedom of the colonies. How far did he promote their constitutional liberty or self-government, and has he a claim to be considered a forerunner of Durham? These questions are natural since he came into intimate contact with the problem of colonial autonomy. When in August 1827 he entered the Colonial Office, he was confronted with those difficulties in the administration of the Canadas which eventually ripened into the rebellion of 1837–8. Durham's historic mission came just ten years after Huskisson held the Secretaryship of State for the Colonies, but the perplexing problems in the government of the Canadian provinces described by Durham faced Huskisson in 1827–8. It is most important to illustrate his attitude towards them and to show that the Liberalism championed in economic policy did not desert him when

[1] *Report*, vol. ii. 243 (Lucas ed., Oxford, 1912).

he came to deal with the constitutional questions of the Empire. The two Canadas contained the largest white population in Britain's second Empire, and the real issue in their administration was the issue that the American Revolution had left unsolved and upon the solution of which the fate of the Empire was finally to rest: the reconciliation of the claims of a self-conscious colony with those of an imperial sovereign.

The constitution obtained by the Canadas in 1791 proved the fertile source of friction between them and the mother country. It was fashioned in that period of reaction which followed upon the American Revolution, and synchronized with the French wars. One lesson the American declaration of independence taught British statesmen; viz. that in the government of colonies democratic institutions should be avoided, and the events in revolutionary France seemed to confirm the lesson. It was generally believed that the thirteen colonies seceded because the monarchial and aristocratic elements were not sufficiently strong in their constitutions. Pitt and his colleagues in the establishment of a government for the Canadas were determined to remedy this defect. In 1789 Grenville, who had charge of colonial affairs wrote to Governor Dorchester that the general object of the new plan of government was 'to assimilate the constitution of the province to that of Britain, as nearly as the difference arising from the measures of the people and the situation of the provinces will admit'. [1] The debate upon the measure throws even a clearer light upon this endeavour of the British ministry. The aim of the Constitutional Bill, remarked Pitt, was to 'bring the government of the province as near as the nature and situation of it would admit to the British constitution'.[2] And of course the British constitution had enough aristocratic and monarchial elements to provide security against the storms of revolution. An intimate part of this assimilative policy was the division of

[1] Grenville to Dorchester, 20 October 1789, Kennedy, *Documents of the Canadian Constitution*, 197 (Oxford, 1918).

[2] *Parliamentary History of England*, 28. 1376.

Canada into two provinces, with separate governments for each. Pitt hopefully believed that such a division as would leave the French dominant in one area and the English in another would enable the French to appreciate at leisure all the benefits of British institutions, and hence become more loyal subjects of the Crown.

Pitt's policy was both right and wrong. It was obviously the only way in which the French could become thoroughly acquainted with British institutions, but since there were also English in the lower province it gave opportunity for racial strife between the two peoples for the control of the representative institutions. In this strife French-Canadian nationality had its birth, and proved a decidedly disturbing factor in the relationship of the province with the Empire. The complete assimilation sought by Pitt remained a dream.

To each province was given a bicameral legislature. A Legislative Assembly represented the people, and was the counterpart of the House of Commons in Britain. A nominated Legislative Council, the members of which held seats for life, exercised somewhat similar functions to the House of Lords. The men appointed to the Legislative Council were to constitute the nucleus of a colonial, hereditary aristocracy and act as a breakwater to the democratic tendencies in American life. Nominal and active executive power in each province was entrusted to a Lieutenant-Governor, who represented His Majesty. He was guided by dispatches from the imperial ministry and was to consider himself responsible to that ministry for the administration of the colony. He was assisted by an executive council appointed on his nomination and responsible to him. This machinery of government, with its irresponsible executive, was not long in operation until it gave rise to friction between the colonists in the Assembly and the imperial authority represented by the Lieutenant-Governor. It worked with ever increasing friction in Lower Canada, where the defects in constitutional machinery were accentuated by the presence of a vigilant French-Canadian populace suspicious of their English administrators.

An adequate account of this strife lies outside the scope of this study, but for a clear understanding of the problem that faced Huskisson a few remarks must be attempted. The most serious trouble developed out of the relationship between the executive and the legislature. While Pitt and his colleagues were sincere in their wish to grant generous representative institutions to the colonists, they never dreamed of resigning final responsibility for the government of the provinces, and it was understood that through the executive authority the will of the Imperial Government was to be exercised. Portland, Minister for the Colonies in 1795, stated the fact very clearly in a letter to Lieutenant-Governor Simcoe of Upper Canada. The legislative power, he observed, being given up to the colonial assembly, 'it is only through the executive power, vested in the person having the government of the province, that the sway of this country can be exercised.'[1] This was a delicate apportionment of authority, but unfortunately it did not satisfy the Assembly. The majority of its members felt that they came together for the government of the province, and so long as they lacked control over matters managed by the executive authority their power was incomplete. When the actions of the administration irritated them, which occurred often enough, they determined that everything vital should be brought under their direction. Thus the real issue at stake was responsible government. Was the Assembly elected by the people or the executive appointed by the Crown to be finally responsible for the government of the province?

Other defects and ambiguities in the Canada Act became apparent. In both provinces conflict over legislation arose between the nominated Legislative Council and the elected Assembly. The Council was composed largely of the permanent official clique whose interests conflicted with those of the people's representatives, and it vetoed the measures of the Assembly without reason or restraint. Troublesome doubts reigned as to the proper procedure in Money Bills and the relative powers of the two chambers

[1] Kennedy, *Documents of the Canadian Constitution*, 237.

on financial questions. Ambiguity on such matters proved to be the nursing mother of friction. In addition the privileges of the House of Assembly were not clearly defined. On the assumption that it was modelled on the House of Commons, it laid claims to the privileges of that ancient chamber, which accentuated strife with the administration. Moreover, the Assembly saw the strategic value of its power to vote supplies. It endeavoured to force the executive to terms by withholding money grants and by demanding complete control over all revenue.

In Lower Canada events hurried to a crisis during Lord Dalhousie's administration, 1820–8, and this crisis faced Huskisson in the Colonial Office. From the outset of his régime Dalhousie was in conflict with the Assembly over finance. In keeping with his instructions from London, he sought a permanent civil list for the judges and officials, but the Assembly, conscious that their strength lay in the power of granting money, were unyielding in their opposition to the vote of a permanent list, particularly as part of the revenue was not under their control. British precedent for a civil list, they argued, was not applicable, for the civil list was but a small item in Britain's expenditure, and whether it was voted permanently or not was of little consequence to the House of Commons. In the colony the annual vote was the sole means of controlling the executive.[1] Notwithstanding Dalhousie's plea that he merely sought permanent provision for permanent expenditure, the Assembly with its majority of French under the ardent leadership of Papineau hardened its heart, and in the spirit of Vane and Pym contended for what it considered its constitutional rights.

In 1827 the storm burst. In the elections of that year Papineau and his followers abused the Governor with indecent extravagance. They described him as embezzling the public funds, blocking all legislation in the Assembly, and deceiving the Colonial Office. Dalhousie retaliated by refusing Papineau as Speaker, although he was elected by

1 Address to His Majesty enclosed in Dalhousie to Bathurst, 25 Jan. 1822. Series Q. 161, p. 50 (Canadian Archives).

the Assembly. One of Dalhousie's early communications to Huskisson as minister informed him of this action. The Assembly promptly re-elected Papineau, and in an endeavour to control the situation Dalhousie prorogued the House. The province then became a hive of excitement. The Colonial Office was showered with dispatches from the popular party and from the Governor and his friends. Not content to rely on correspondence the Assembly sent over three representatives, Neilson, Viger, and Cuvillier, to plead their case and to interview Huskisson in person. These brought petitions signed in various sections of the province which emphasized what the petitioners considered the rightful demand of the Assembly to control revenue. They complained that 'in this province of the British Empire large sums of public money of the revenue levied within this province, have been applied, year after year, by warrant of the executive government, without any appropriation by the legislature of the province.' [1]

They had other grounds for discontent. The Legislative Council was an object of criticism. They considered that it violated the spirit of the law of the English constitution:

> 'The majority of its members, consisting of persons whose principal resources for the support of themselves and their families are the salaries, emoluments, and fees derived from office which they hold during pleasure, are interested in maintaining and increasing the salaries, emoluments, and fees of public offices paid by the people, and also in supporting divers abuses favourable to persons holding offices.' [2]

Nor did the Governor escape a slating. His refusal to accept the Speaker elected by the Assembly and his prorogation of the provincial parliament were both denounced. The petitioners implied that his administration was responible for neglect in the settlement of the waste lands, and for the general commercial depression in the province. On the other hand, Huskisson was certainly in no danger of condemning Dalhousie unheard, for the latter in lengthy

[1] See petition of the counties in the district of Quebec and of the county of Warwick, district of Montreal, Series Q. 184, p. 71, p. 12 (Canadian Archives).

[2] *Ibid.* p. 5.

dispatches met and repudiated the accusations of his opponents. He claimed that the petitions did not contain the real sentiments of the province but only the opinions of agitators. He considered that the chief existing evil was the ascendancy of the French in the Assembly. Hence he recommended that the Constitutional Act of 1791 be so amended as to alter the boundaries of the counties in order to give a more adequate representation to the British. The main object of his suggestions was 'to infuse into the representative body such a portion of English feeling and liberal ideas, as shall make it conformable to the views of the statesmen who in 1791 framed and carried through Parliament the existing Constitutional Act.' [1] But Dalhousie was not content with dispatches. He sent over a Montreal barrister and magistrate, Gale, to represent his views, and to prevent Neilson and his friends from throwing dust in Huskisson's eyes.

The attitude of Huskisson towards the situation is not difficult to follow. From the outset he had sympathy with the popular demands; and the representatives of the Lower Canadian Assembly found him kindly and attentive. To him their case seemed plausible. On learning of Dalhousie's dismissal of Papineau as Speaker, he wrote regretting that the Governor had exercised his prerogative on such a matter, and later he recalled Dalhousie although not censuring him. He fully sympathized with the claim of the Assembly for control over the provincial revenue. When Dalhousie's emissary, Gale, appeared before him, Huskisson showed him the complaints of the Canadian leaders and remarked, 'What defence can be made against charges like these? A British House of Commons will always support the control of the Assembly over the public monies.' [2] He viewed the struggle from the same angle as the colonial reformers, that of British precedents, and came to the same conclusion. But Gale reported that he

[1] Dalhousie to Huskisson, 25 January 1828. Series Q. 182, pt. 1, p. 12 (Canadian Archives).

[2] Gale to Cochran, 13 June 1828 (Dalhousie Papers, Canadian Archives).

had done his best and with some success to convince Huskisson that the colonial struggle was not simply between the administration on the one side and the people on the other as had been represented, but was in fact between two different portions of the population, one of which endeavoured to establish an anti-English system. Gale was certainly influential in his pleading, for Huskisson came gradually to the conclusion that the situation in the Canadas was far more complex than he had at first thought and that it required thorough investigation by Parliament. Previous colonial secretaries were content to accept the information sent them by the Governors, and to frame their policy upon it. But Huskisson believed that both sides of the colonial controversy must be thoroughly investigated, and a policy arrived at based on the conclusions of the investigation. He realized the gravity of the situation and was not prepared to take action until the whole question had been carefully examined by Parliament. Hence on 2 May 1828 he moved for the appointment of a select committee to inquire into the state of the civil government of Canada. His speech on the occasion was one of his greatest utterances on imperial questions, and was the fullest statement of his faith in Britain's colonial possessions.[1]

He surveyed the causes of strife in the Canadas and expressed his desire to do justice to all parties. On the two most vexatious problems—the struggle between the French and the English and that between the executive and the legislature—he made interesting pronouncements. He showed sympathy with the English in the lower province, especially with their complaints that they were living in a community where only ancient French customs and French law prevailed: 'The result is, that Englishmen in Canada are as much like aliens and settlers in a foreign land, as an equal number of British subjects, who should have sat down in the centre of France in the thirteenth century.'[2] Although he had personally no ready-made panaceas for the situation, he was convinced that those suggested, such as the union of the upper and lower provinces, were open to

[1] *Speeches*, iii. 268. [2] *Ibid.* 279.

many objections. He looked to the select committee to discover a solution. Huskisson was no Durham. While sympathizing with the minority of English in the lower provinces, he was not prepared to recommend an anglifying policy, and certainly frowned upon the idea of a union of the provinces. On the struggle of the executive and legislature over revenue his views were more positive. He believed that although the legislature had little legal foundation for their claim to a complete control over provincial revenues, it would be wise to concede it, provided that a permanent civil list were established for the maintenance of the judicial and other departments.

The significance of Huskisson's speech lies not with his positive suggestions but with his uncertainty as to the right policy. The audacity that marked his attitude towards the navigation laws is absent. On the problem of colonial government he lacked those definite convictions which led him to attack mercantile regulations. His robust faith in free enterprise and his firm grasp of classical economics availed little in deciding how much political power a colonial legislature should possess. Durham ten years later was forced to a solution for colonial difficulties by his enthusiasm for self-government, but that enthusiasm is only slightly evident in Huskisson. We should not perhaps expect it in him. After all he could not elude his period and its tendencies. The first fifteen years after Waterloo were an era of reconstruction without zeal for self-government. That zeal was a development of the thirties. Huskisson left the framing of a policy to the select committee, trustful that after a thorough investigation they would know best what to recommend. Under the circumstances his action was wise, but it satisfied neither party in the colony. Gale felt that Huskisson was mindful of a discontented body of English within the French province, but he was 'greatly disappointed at the want of energy or timidity in Mr. Huskisson in throwing the responsibility of measures from the minister on Parliament.' [1] On the other hand, the *Quebec Gazette*, which

1 Gale to Cochran, 13 June 1828 (Dalhousie Papers, Canadian Archives).

represented the opinions of the reformers in the colony, strongly disapproved of Huskisson's suggestions as inadequate. It suspected that Huskisson was unduly concerned with the plight of the English Canadians. It noted with some regret that he ridiculed French land laws, and that he declared that as long as England retained Canada, it was her duty to 'imbue it with English feeling and benefit it with English laws and institutions'. Such a statement did not indicate that Huskisson was sufficiently considerate of His Majesty's French-Canadian subjects. Yet the *Gazette* was prepared to trust the man who had given to the colonies freedom of trade.[1]

Huskisson's select committee met, carried out a careful investigation, and made a report upon all the vital matters that pertained to the government and welfare of the province.[2] Upon the question in dispute between the Assembly and the Executive, the control of public revenue, the committee followed the recommendation of Huskisson, that 'the real interests of the province would be best promoted by placing the receipt and expenditure of the whole public revenue under the superintendence and control of the House of Assembly'. While this concession should be made, the Governor, the members of the Executive Council, and the judges should be rendered independent of the annual votes of the House of Assembly by a permanent civil list. Other valuable recommendations were made on the thorny problems in dispute. Discussion of them would draw one far afield from Huskisson. While few of the recommendations were immediately carried into effect, they remained as safe guide-posts to the colonial and imperial governments. The report amply justified Huskisson in appointing the committee, and it adequately represented the Liberal views of himself and his followers. It was received by the Assembly in Lower Canada as an 'imperishable monument of justice and profound wisdom',

[1] *Quebec Gazette*, 16 June 1828.

[2] *Report and Evidence of the Select Committee on the State of Civil Government of Lower Canada* (British Parliamentary Papers, 1828, vol. vii).

which is probably sufficient testimony to its Liberalism.[1] Yet while Liberal and holding out the open hand of concession, it was no elaborate championship of colonial political liberty. It is scarcely extravagant to say that it was fully expressive of the restraint of Huskisson's Liberal creed. In his brief stay at the Colonial Office he was not prepared to attempt what Durham, Russell, and Grey later accomplished. The opportunity had not yet arrived. His was a policy, infused with the compromise of a transitional period.

With the Canada Committee the colonial policy of Huskisson came to an end. Indeed before the committee's report appeared Huskisson had resigned from Wellington's ministry, and had therefore no opportunity to attempt to carry into effect its recommendations.

[1] See the address of the Assembly to the Governor in Christie, R., *A History of the Late Province of Lower Canada*, iii. 222 (Montreal, 1866).

CONCLUSION

NO extended conclusion is necessary to this study of Huskisson. Preceding chapters have shown the place that he held in the dawn of nineteenth-century reform that began in 1822 and ended with the death of Canning. The unifying thread in the reforms of the Huskisson-Canningite régime is obvious. The principles that actuated Huskisson and his associates were those of the economists. Every period of reform has in the background its school of abstract thought, and Adam Smith and his successors were the fountain source of the ideas of early English Liberalism. The current political economy undermined mercantilism in theory; Huskisson attacked it in fact. He did not see eye to eye with Ricardo and M'Culloch, and on some questions departed sharply from their recommendations, but he had their general outlook and accepted their principles. He attacked the high fiscal protection of mercantilism, its narrow economic nationalism, and in minor ways its direction of economic life by the organs of political life. His policy translated the ideas of the classical economists into the active language of the statute book with such modifications as a statesman had a licence to introduce. Smith had no disciple more true to his doctrines in the sphere of statesmanship. Little wonder that his High Tory opponents should bracket together atheism and political economy as the two destructive agencies in society, for political economy was the leaven of the age. The author of *The Wealth of Nations* despaired of free trade in the England of his day, because of (i) public prejudice, and (ii) private interests. By his gradual steps in reform Huskisson did something to overcome the former and to conciliate the latter. He even expressed his political faith in sentences that might readily be mistaken for Smith's: 'To leave to individuals to follow their own views, to regulate their own speculations, and to consult their own interests. This I consider to be a general rule, applicable alike to the industry and commerce of the country.'

With Huskisson's economic creed there was blended a strong national and imperial sentiment, evident in much of his legislation. This sentiment combined with a natural restraint kept him from going far along the path of *laisser-faire*. The Manchester school which carried free trade policy to completion could scarcely claim Huskisson as one of their number. Most of them were 'little Englanders', who rejected Empire because it presented no profits. Huskisson did not share such a view. He lacked the bleak utilitarianism that characterized many of his contemporaries in the task of reform. He was not narrowed by the Benthamite influence, so strong in his age. His often quoted sentence from the speech on the Canada question embodied his creed: 'England cannot afford to be little. She must be what she is, or nothing.' In his pride of Empire he was divorced from Ricardo and his school, but akin to Adam Smith who recognized imperialism and had written his faith in patriotism: 'We do not love our country merely as part of the great society of mankind; we love it for its own sake and independently of any such consideration.' It was also Smith who argued that the larger issues of Empire were not embraced in a consideration of profits or revenue, but extended far beyond them. His philosophy was that of Huskisson, who realized that every question could not be subjected to an economic test. Illustrations of this belief abound. In 1823 in a debate on the West Indian sugar duties Ricardo argued as if the only vital question was 'where, as consumers, could we get our sugar at the cheapest'. Huskisson strongly objecting to such a test, pleaded that the question must be examined with reference to a number of complicated circumstances. The whole problem of general imperial interest was involved.

Though he had confidence in the freedom of private enterprise, he nevertheless believed that state intervention for humanitarian reasons was always justifiable. As he retorted to Hume in a debate already described, he was unable to understand the nature of those pure abstract principles which prevented intervention where the interests of humanity were at stake. He had nothing of that rigid doctrinaire attitude which later led the Manchester school to oppose factory legislation on the ground that it infringed a principle. Non-intervention with them was a fetish. With Huskisson it was an economic policy aerated with humanity. But his humanitarianism itself was seasoned by common sense, as his position on slavery showed.

In preceding chapters something has been said of the effects of Huskisson's reforms. Here only a few summarizing remarks need be made. The policy of the reciprocity treaties undoubtedly facilitated and helped to extend British commerce. Its precise influence cannot be determined, because in that age as in every other, diverse influences affected the volume of trade. At the very least the reciprocity treaties warded off harsh retaliatory enactments by the European states. Huskisson's tariff changes did not prove equally influential. They were meant to wean continental powers from prohibitions and high protection, but the principal governments clung to their protectionist tariffs, and British industries obtained no benefit in this direction. Larger markets were not found in Europe but in the tropical and sub-tropical portions of the Empire, where Lancashire goods entered without tariff hindrance. The fiscal changes also failed to reduce smuggling. Indeed, as pointed out, the smuggling of silks seems to have increased. Yet the introduction of competition to the home market exercised a stimulating effect on British manufactures. Witness is borne to the fact by the developments in the silk industry. Enough has been said in a preceding chapter on the effects of changes in the navigation laws. How much of the increase in British shipping was due directly to the changes cannot be determined. But the increase appeared sufficiently great to convince ministers in 1849 that everything was to be gained by the total repeal of the laws. Huskisson's changes in the old colonial system must be defended on the ground that the need for them had arrived, and that for the time being they met the requirements of colonial opinion, although they stopped short of what that opinion demanded in the forties. Similarly Huskisson's corn law policy was an attempt to meet the needs of industrial Britain without too great a sacrifice of the agricultural interests. Its effect was to make easy the transition from protection to freedom in corn imports.

With no biographical aims in view we have said little of the man himself, and in conclusion only a few comments are necessary. His physical appearance was described by Greville as

'tall, slouchy, and ignoble-looking. In society he was extremely agreeable, without much animation, generally cheerful, with a great deal of humour, information and anecdote, gentlemanlike, unassuming, slow in speech, and with a downcast look, as if he avoided meeting anybody's gaze. . . . It is probably true that there is no man in Parliament or perhaps out of it, so well versed in finance, commerce, trade, and colonial matters.' [1]

Others speak of his lack of personal warmth, but apparently he was not much handicapped by it for he won great popularity. His receptions at Liverpool were comparable to those which a prime minister might receive, and his former constituents, at Chichester, showed no less devotion. His oratory was not in the strain of his brilliant colleague Canning. It had none of the latter's flights and rhythmic perorations, but was weighty in argument and evidence. His parliamentary speeches were always received with careful attention, and generally stirred up comment, critical or laudatory, outside the walls of Parliament. His energy was repeatedly spoken of by his contemporaries, and found expression in the support of many movements concerned with the shaping of the new generation. He took a ready interest in the building of the Liverpool and Manchester railway, the opening of which witnessed his tragic death. Not merely railway construction but another infant undertaking, steam navigation, won his hearty support. At the time of his death he was assisting in the promotion of a plan sponsored by Sir James Carnegie to establish steam navigation between Liverpool and America. He looked upon it as an agent of great value in developing that overseas trade which his reforms were designed to encourage.

[1] *Memoirs* (1875), 397–8.

It may well be emphasized in conclusion that such position as Huskisson has attained in British history is due in large part to his definitely English temperament and to the fact that he shared in a great, creative tradition—a reformer in lineal descent from the younger Pitt and closely in line with his distinguished successors, Peel and Gladstone. He had the Englishman's pragmatic method and pronounced mistrust of an *a priori* point of view. This fact deserves the more attention because, as disclosed in previous chapters, Huskisson was under the sway of current economic thought. But he never lost himself in the misty uplands of theory, and while he might allow an abstract doctrine to influence him he did not fail to bring it to the bar of political and economic facts. It is impossible to read his speeches or to study the details of his public life without being convinced that he was essentially a realistic, not a doctrinaire reformer. The logic of realities was more powerful with him than all the seductive attractions of abstract reasoning. He tackled closely and boldly the problems of his age. His policy neither lagged behind nor advanced far ahead of the existing needs of England, but marched in happy unison with them. He had no wish to hurry the years. He left time to bring its own new policies as social requirements demanded. His wisdom was the wisdom of England. His achievements were those of a statesman thoroughly representative of his race, and one may venture the judgement that no other type of statesman could have assisted better in piloting the state through the perilous rocks and shoals that confronted it between 1815–30.

INDEX

For Product Safety Concerns and Information please contact our EU representative GPSR@taylorandfrancis.com Taylor & Francis Verlag GmbH, Kaufingerstraße 24, 80331 München, Germany